If
God
Is
Good
Study Guide

RANDY ALCORN

MULTNOMAH
BOOKS

IF GOD IS GOOD STUDY GUIDE
PUBLISHED BY MULTNOMAH BOOKS
12265 Oracle Boulevard, Suite 200
Colorado Springs, Colorado 80921

Italics in Scripture quotations reflect the author's added emphasis.

Portions of this study guide have been adapted from *If God Is Good,* copyright © 2009 by Eternal Perspective Ministries, published by Multnomah Books.

Trade Paperback ISBN 978-1-60142-345-0
eBook ISBN 978-1-60142-351-1

Published in the United States by WaterBrook Multnomah, an imprint of the Crown Publishing Group, a division of Penguin Random House LLC, New York.

MULTNOMAH and its mountain colophon are registered trademarks of Penguin Random House LLC.

147429898

Contents

PART 4
Our Best Response

Introduction

Three Ways to Use This Study Guide

Welcome to an exploration of the vital and universal themes that are discussed in Randy Alcorn's book *If God Is Good*.

This study guide will be the most help to you if you're going through it as part of a small group or class (see the "Group Leaders' Guide" at the back of this book). But of course you can benefit greatly from going through it on your own as well.

What's Here?
This is a thorough guide to a fairly large book, but the structure is simple. This guide includes components and questions that link to each chapter in *IGIG*. You'll see four elements here for each *IGIG* chapter, marked by these four headings:

          ❋ Focus In
          ❋ Interact
        ❋ ❋ Explore Further
      ❋ ❋ ● Investigate Deeper

    ❋ *Focus In*—This component briefly highlights a few of the most important points made in the *IGIG* chapter. Reading this will get you "warmed up" to the topic.

    ❋ *Interact*—Here you'll find a few brief excerpts reprinted from the *IGIG* chapter, and each excerpt is followed by a question to help you interact with it.

* * *Explore Further*—These questions help you reflect further
    on the chapter's topic, and they often direct you back into
    the pages of *IGIG* to scan the chapter and look for certain
    things.
* * • *Investigate Deeper*—These are the most comprehensive
    questions; they assume you are fully acquainted with the
    IGIG chapter's content.

You'll see subheadings throughout this study guide that tell you
which chapter in *IGIG* these elements correspond to, so you may easily
go back and forth from the book to the study guide.

The Pace and Approach

This companion guide to *IGIG* is designed for use in a variety of ways.
Choose which best suits your schedule.

We suggest you follow one of three approaches:

* *Overview*—This is designed as a **four-week course.** You'll
    notice from the contents page that this guide is divided
    into four parts; in this overview approach, you study one
    part each week. (As you do, complete everything under
    the "* Focus In" and "* Interact" headings, but skip all
    the rest.)
* * *Exploratory*—Here we suggest an **eight-week course.** With
    this simple structure, each of the four main parts is split in
    two—with an "A" unit and a "B" unit. So alternate each
    week between units A and B until all four parts are com-
    pleted. (You'll complete "* Focus In" and "* Interact"
    and also the questions under the "* * Explore Further"
    heading.)
* * • *Intensive*—This is a suggested **thirteen-week course**
    linked closely to the structure of *IGIG,* which includes an
    introduction, eleven sections, and a conclusion (1 + 11 +
    1 = 13). You'll see headings here in the study guide text
    that exactly match those section headings in *IGIG.* (In
    this intensive approach, you'll complete everything in this

study guide—not only the elements mentioned above, but also everything under the "⁎ ⁎ • Investigate Deeper" heading for each chapter.)

You'll notice that the number of "bullets" you see helps you remember which elements in the study guide go with which approach:

⁎ *Overview* (four weeks): Do everything under any heading that has a single bullet (⁎), and skip the rest.

⁎ ⁎ *Exploratory* (eight weeks): Complete *both* the single-bullet *and* the double-bullet (⁎ ⁎) sections, and skip the rest.

⁎ ⁎ • *Intensive* (thirteen weeks): Complete *everything*— including the triple-bullet (⁎ ⁎ •) sections.

Summary: The Three Approaches

To summarize, here are the three approaches we suggest:

OVERVIEW
(FOUR WEEKS)

Each week you'll do one of the four main parts in this study guide:

Week One—*Part 1:* The Burning Question

Week Two—*Part 2:* Our Search for Solutions

Week Three—*Part 3:* God at Work

Week Four—*Part 4:* Our Best Response

Within each of these parts, you'll do everything under any heading that has a single bullet (⁎) and skip the rest.

EXPLORATORY
(EIGHT WEEKS)

Each week you'll do half of each main part in this study guide:

Week One—*1-A:* Something's Wrong

Week Two—*1-B:* Tragic Choices

Week Three—*2-A:* Alternative Answers

Week Four—*2-B:* The Great Drama

Week Five—*3-A:* Who's in Control?
Week Six—*3-B:* Eternal Perspectives
Week Seven—*4-A:* Accepting God's Purposes
Week Eight—*4-B:* What We Can Do
Within each of these parts, you'll **complete *both* the single-bullet (◦)** *and* **the double-bullet (◦◦) sections** and skip the rest.

INTENSIVE (THIRTEEN WEEKS)

Each week, you'll complete the study guide contents that correspond to each of the numbered sections in *IGIG* (you'll see the headings clearly marked within the study guide text):

Week One—Facing the Hurt and Confusion (corresponds to the introduction in *IGIG*)

Week Two—*Section 1:* Understanding the Problem of Evil and Suffering

Week Three—*Section 2:* Understanding Evil: Its Origins, Nature, and Consequences

Week Four—*Section 3:* Problems for Non-Theists: Moral Standards, Goodness, and Extreme Evil

Week Five—*Section 4:* Proposed Solutions to the Problem of Evil and Suffering: Limiting God's Attributes

Week Six—*Section 5:* Evil and Suffering in the Great Drama of Christ's Redemptive Work

Week Seven—*Section 6:* Divine Sovereignty and Meaningful Human Choice: Accounting for Evil and Suffering

Week Eight—*Section 7:* The Two Eternal Solutions to the Problem of Evil: Heaven and Hell

Week Nine—*Section 8:* God's Allowance and Restraint of Evil and Suffering

Week Ten—*Section 9:* Evil and Suffering Used for God's Glory

Week Eleven—*Section 10:* Why Does God Allow Suffering?

Week Twelve—*Section 11:* Living Meaningfully in Suffering

<u>Week Thirteen</u>—Final Thoughts About God, Goodness, Evil,
  and Suffering (*IGIG* conclusion)

Throughout these weekly assignments, you'll **complete everything**—
including the triple-bullet (◦ ◦ ●) sections.

At a Glance

Here's a chart to help you remember the week-by-week structure, depending on which approach you choose:

Study Guide Structure	Links to These Sections in the *IGIG* Book	4-Week Track (Overview)	8-Week Track (Exploratory)	13-Week Track (Intensive)
Part 1: The Burning Question		Week 1		
1-A: Something's Wrong	*Introduction:* A Note to Readers, Especially to Those Hurting and Confused		Week 1	Week 1
	Section 1: Understanding the Problem of Evil and Suffering			Week 2
1-B: Tragic Choices	*Section 2:* Understanding Evil: Its Origins, Nature, and Consequences		Week 2	Week 3

Study Guide Structure	Links to These Sections in the *IGIG* Book	4-Week Track (Overview)	8-Week Track (Exploratory)	13-Week Track (Intensive)
Part 2: Our Search for Solutions		Week 2		
2-A: Alternative Answers	*Section 3:* Problems for Non-Theists: Moral Standards, Goodness, and Extreme Evil		Week 3	Week 4
	Section 4: Proposed Solutions to the Problem of Evil and Suffering: Limiting God's Attributes			Week 5
2-B: The Great Drama	*Section 5:* Evil and Suffering in the Great Drama of Christ's Redemptive Work		Week 4	Week 6

Study Guide Structure	Links to These Sections in the *IGIG* Book	4-Week Track (Overview)	8-Week Track (Exploratory)	13-Week Track (Intensive)
Part 3: God at Work		Week 3		
3-A: Who's in Control?	*Section 6:* Divine Sovereignty and Meaningful Human Choice: Accounting for Evil and Suffering		Week 5	Week 7
3-B: Eternal Perspectives	*Section 7:* The Two Eternal Solutions to the Problem of Evil: Heaven and Hell		Week 6	Week 8
	Section 8: God's Allowance and Restraint of Evil and Suffering			Week 9

Study Guide Structure	Links to These Sections in the *IGIG* Book	4-Week Track (Overview)	8-Week Track (Exploratory)	13-Week Track (Intensive)
Part 4: Our Best Response		Week 4		
4-A: Accepting God's Purposes	*Section 9:* Evil and Suffering Used for God's Glory		Week 7	Week 10
	Section 10: Why Does God Allow Suffering?			Week 11
4-B: What We Can Do	*Section 11:* Living Meaningfully in Suffering		Week 8	Week 12
	Conclusion: Final Thoughts About God, Goodness, Evil, and Suffering			Week 13

PART I

The Burning Question

(Links with the introduction and sections 1–2 in If God Is Good, pages 1–92)

1-A

Something's Wrong

FACING THE HURT AND CONFUSION

(Links with the introduction in *If God Is Good,* pages 1–5.)
Again, a quick reminder: Here and throughout this study guide…

- *if you're following the less intensive overview approach* (typically a four-week course), do all the sections that begin with a single-bullet (◉) heading.
- *if you're pursuing the more exploratory approach* (typically eight weeks), complete *both* the single-bullet *and* the double-bullet (◉◉) sections.
- *if you're taking the most intensive approach* (thirteen weeks), complete *everything*—including the triple-bullet (◉◉●) sections.

Review the introduction for more details.

◉ FOCUS IN

Our outlook on God and the world around us will be radically affected by how we answer this question: if God is good…*why all this evil and suffering?*

In our search for answers, all of us bring our own burdens to the journey—burdens that can shake our faith to the core. Meanwhile, to find the right perspectives as we try to make sense of life, we need to let our thinking be shaped by the truth of God's Word.

◉ INTERACT

Think about your own experiences and perspectives regarding evil and suffering as you read the following brief excerpt from Randy Alcorn's *If*

God Is Good. (Throughout this study guide, all the excerpts from Randy's book will be set off with pointers (» «), like the quote below. Each time you see that mark, read the excerpt, think about it, and then respond to the question that follows.)

> » How we answer this book's central question will radically affect how we see God and the world around us.
>
> We may want to turn away from world suffering and refuse to reflect on the significance of our own pain; we just want it to go away. But despite the superficiality of our culture, we remain God's image-bearers—thinking and caring people, wired to ask questions and seek answers.
>
> No question looms larger than the central question of this book: If God is good...*why all this evil and suffering?* If God loves us, how can he justify allowing (or sending) the sometimes overwhelming difficulties we face?
>
> Does this great question interest you? If so, I invite you to join me on a journey of discovery. «

1. How would you describe your own interests and concerns regarding this topic? Why is that "central question" Randy mentioned an important issue for you personally?

> » While traveling this long road (researching what Scripture says about evil and suffering), I found something surprising: the journey was not only rewarding, but fascinating, enlightening, and at times downright enjoyable. I know it sounds counterintuitive—shouldn't it depress someone to meditate on evil and suffering? In fact, I'd already seen enough evil and suffering to feel deeply troubled. What I needed was perspective. Instead of being disheartened, I'm encouraged.
>
> In this process, I've taken the most pleasure in focusing on God, exploring his attributes of goodness, love, holiness, justice, patience, grace, and mercy. While my journey

hasn't unearthed easy answers, I'm astonished at how much insight Scripture offers. ❖

2. To what extent do you share with Randy the sense of being "deeply troubled" by the evil and suffering you've seen?

❖ We each bring our own burdens on the journey.

If abuse, rape, desertion, paralysis, debilitating disease, or the loss of a loved one has devastated you, then this issue isn't theoretical, philosophical, or theological. It's deeply personal. Logical arguments won't satisfy you; in fact, they might offend you. You need help with the *emotional* problem of evil, not merely the *logical* problem of evil.

Though I write personally, from the heart, and tell stories of great courage and perspective, I must also present a case from Scripture and appeal to logic. But remember this: you are a whole person, and the path to your heart travels through your mind. Truth matters. To touch us at the heart level—and to keep touching us over days, months, years, and decades—truth must work its way into our *minds.* ❖

3. Randy mentions approaching this topic *emotionally,* as well as *logically* and *scripturally.* For you personally, what part does God's Word play in your understanding of absolute truth?

◉● EXPLORE FURTHER

(For more exploration, notice the **bold-text** sentences as you page through *IGIG*'s introduction, and read them over. Take time to stop and read the continuing paragraphs that interest you most. Then respond to the questions below.)

4. Glance over the text of the *IGIG* introduction, look for the following quoted scriptures, and highlight or underline

them (or you can simply look them up in your own Bible): Exodus 3:7 and 1 Peter 1:7. Together, what perspective from God do these two verses give us about this topic of evil and suffering?

5. Look also at these two quoted scriptures in the *IGIG* introduction: 2 Timothy 3:16 and Isaiah 55:11. How do they reinforce your need to have true biblical convictions and perspectives on this sometimes confusing and disturbing topic?

6. What do you need to understand more thoroughly in order to trust and accept God's goodness in the face of the world's suffering and evil?

7. As you look over the bold-text statements in *IGIG*'s introduction, which one do you think is most important right now, and why?

● ● ● INVESTIGATE DEEPER

(For more intensive study, first read through all of the *IGIG* introduction. Then answer the questions below.)

8. Randy writes in *IGIG* that he desires for God to "give us the strength to face a world that is not what it once was, or what it one day will be" (page 5). How would you explain those phrases about the world from your own understanding of biblical teaching?

9. Which stories or illustrations in the *IGIG* introduction did you find yourself most drawn to, and why? How were they helpful for you?

10. Look up these scriptures in your own Bible, and record the truths you find regarding this topic of suffering, evil, and God: Judges 10:16 and Revelation 21:4.

Understanding the Problem of Evil and Suffering

(Links with section 1 in *If God Is Good,* pages 7–44.)

Why Is the Problem of Evil and Suffering So Important?
(See also chapter 1 in *IGIG,* page 9.)

◈ FOCUS IN
People point to the problem of evil and suffering as their greatest reason for not believing in God—it's not merely *a* problem, it's *the* problem. In almost any serious conversation about Christianity with those who reject it, you're likely to hear the problem of evil raised. It looms as a seemingly insurmountable barrier to accepting the existence of the kind of wise, loving, sovereign God proclaimed by Christians.

Suffering and evil exert a force that either pushes us away from God or pulls us toward him. If you base your faith in God on lack of affliction, your faith lives on the brink of extinction and is liable to collapse with the news of a frightening diagnosis or a shattering phone call. Token, fairweather faith will not survive suffering, nor should it.

◈ INTERACT
(As before, read each *IGIG* excerpt, and then answer the question that follows.)

If we open our eyes, we'll see the problem of evil and suffering even when it doesn't touch us directly....

I once had to tell a wife, son, and daughter that their husband and father had died on a hunting trip. I still remember the anguished face of the little girl, then hearing her wail, "Not Daddy, no, not Daddy!"

Years ago I had to tell my mother that her only brother had been murdered with a meat cleaver.

A Christian woman tipped over on her riding lawn mower and fell into a pond. The machine landed on top of her, pinning her to the bottom and drowning her. Such a bizarre death prompted some to ask, "Why, God?" and "Why like this?"...

Our own suffering is often our wake-up call. But even if you aren't now facing it, look around and you'll see many who are.

1. What current experiences of suffering—either yours or someone's you know—are you most aware of at this time?

More people point to the problem of evil and suffering as their reason for not believing in God than any other—it is not merely *a* problem, it is *the* problem....

You will not get far in a conversation with someone who rejects the Christian faith before the problem of evil is raised. Pulled out like the ultimate trump card, it's supposed to silence believers and prove that the all-good and all-powerful God of the Bible doesn't exist.

2. In your opinion, what is it about the problem of suffering and evil that causes so many people to question or reject either the existence or the goodness of God?

�֎ A faith that leaves us unprepared for suffering is a false faith that deserves to be lost....

Believing God exists is not the same as trusting the God who exists. A nominal Christian often discovers in suffering that his faith has been in his church, denomination, or family tradition, but not Christ. As he faces evil and suffering, he may lose his faith. But that's actually a good thing. I have sympathy for people who lose their faith, but any faith lost in suffering wasn't a faith worth keeping. ֍

3. Do you agree or disagree that "any faith lost in suffering wasn't a faith worth keeping"? Why?

✖ Suffering will come; we owe it to God, ourselves, and those around us to prepare for it.

Live long enough and you *will* suffer. In this life, the only way to avoid suffering is to die....

A young woman battling cancer wrote me, "I was surprised that when it happened, it was hard and it hurt and I was sad and I couldn't find anything good or redeeming about my losses. I never expected that a Christian who had access to God could feel so empty and alone."

Our failure to teach a biblical theology of suffering leaves Christians unprepared for harsh realities. It also leaves our children vulnerable to history, philosophy, and global studies classes that raise the problems of evil and suffering while denying the Christian worldview. Since the question *will* be raised, shouldn't Christian parents and churches raise it first and take people to Scripture to see what God says about it? ֍

4. What are some things that parents or churches could do to better prepare those under their care for handling various experiences of suffering?

● ● **EXPLORE FURTHER**
(For more exploration, look over especially the **bold-text** sentences as you page through *IGIG* chapter 1, read the continuing paragraphs that interest you most, and then answer the following questions.)

5. In the most difficult suffering you've experienced, how prepared were you for it — spiritually, emotionally, mentally, even physically?

6. If you have ever had a serious conversation with anyone about the problem of evil and suffering, how prepared did you feel to tackle the subject? If you haven't, how do you think you would approach it now?

7. On the last page of this chapter, look at these quoted scriptures: Philippians 1:23 and Revelation 21:3–4. How do they affect our perception of suffering?

8. In this chapter of *IGIG,* as you look over the bold-text statements, which one do you think has the most significance for your life, and why?

● ● ● **INVESTIGATE DEEPER**
(For more intensive study, read *IGIG* chapter 1.)

9. What's the best answer to the question in this chapter's title: why is the problem of evil and suffering so important?

10. In what ways is this problem of evil and suffering a "cornerstone" for atheism (see page 11)?

11. Which stories or illustrations in *IGIG* chapter 1 did you find most compelling, and why?

What Is the Problem of Evil and Suffering?
(See also chapter 2 in *IGIG,* page 17.)

⊛ FOCUS IN

If God is all-good, then he must want to prevent evil and suffering. If he is all-knowing, then he must know how to prevent it. If God is all-powerful, then he is able to prevent it. And yet…a great deal of evil and suffering exists. Why?

The problem of evil has found a prominent voice in what may seem the most unlikely place…the Bible. No other book asks so bluntly, passionately, and frequently why God permits evil and why evil people sometimes thrive while the righteous suffer. Barely has the first chapter of the Bible described the original creation—saying, "God saw all that he had made, and it was very good"—before a terrible shadow falls: evil and suffering burst into the world.

⊛ INTERACT

�֎ Philosophers throughout the ages have pondered the problem of evil and suffering.

Three centuries before Christ, the Greek philosopher Epicurus asked, "Whence evil—if there be a God?" In 1776, skeptic David Hume asked a series of questions about God: "Is he willing to prevent evil, but not able? then is he impotent. Is he able, but not willing? then is he malevolent. Is he both able and willing? whence then is evil?"...

Recently I received this e-mail: "I have family members who tell me it is evil and suffering that keeps them from seeing God as good; or if he's good, they say he must not be powerful enough or interested enough to do something about it." Neither the writer of the note nor his family members claim to be philosophers. Nonetheless, they wrestle with exactly the same question: why would a good and all-powerful God permit evil and suffering?

This problem crosses all barriers of time and culture.... The problem of evil is a central theme in human storytelling.

1. What books or films are you familiar with that especially address the problem of evil?

The problem of evil has found a prominent voice in what may seem the most unlikely place...the Bible....

If atheists would read Scripture, they'd find their best arguments articulated there....

The problem of evil lies at the very heart of the biblical account and serves as the crux of the unfolding drama of redemption....

The Bible never sugarcoats evil....

The fact that the Bible raises the problem of evil gives us full permission to do so.

2. From what you know of the Bible, what are some things it says about suffering? What stories of suffering does it tell?

✖ Some perspectives can give great help in dealing with the problem, but none bring neat and tidy solutions....

I've read books by atheists and Holocaust survivors, and have interviewed dozens of men and women who have endured extreme evil and suffering. The more I've done so, the more I've asked God to give me wisdom—and I've discovered that wisdom begins with the humility to say there's a great deal I don't understand. ✖

3. When you think about evil and suffering, what aspects of it cause you to humbly admit (as Randy does), "There's a great deal I don't understand"? What are your most persistent questions in this area?

●● EXPLORE FURTHER

(For more exploration, look over especially the **bold-text** sentences in *IGIG* chapter 2, read the continuing paragraphs that interest you most, and then answer the following questions.)

4. During your years in school, how was the problem of evil and suffering dealt with in the classroom?

5. When has the problem of evil and suffering surfaced in your personal experience, or in that of your family and friends?

6. Glance over the text of *IGIG* chapter 2, looking for and marking the following quoted passages: Revelation 6:10; Habakkuk 1:2–3; Psalms 10:1; 42:9; 44:23–24. What words are used to show the deep disturbance the biblical writers sensed regarding suffering and evil?

7. Based on the scriptures quoted in this chapter—Matthew
   12:39; 6:13; Romans 12:21; Luke 13:27—what is the
   Bible's view of evil?

8. In this chapter of *IGIG,* as you look over the bold-text
   statements, which one has the most significance for your
   life, and why?

●●● INVESTIGATE DEEPER

(For more intensive study, read *IGIG* chapter 2.)

9. What's the best answer to the question in this chapter's
   title: what is the problem of evil and suffering?

10. What convinces you that the Bible addresses the problem
    of evil and suffering with complete candor and openness?

11. Which stories or illustrations in *IGIG* chapter 2 did you
    find yourself most drawn to, and why?

What Is Evil, and How Does It Differ from Suffering?
   (See also chapter 3 in *IGIG,* page 24.)

● FOCUS IN

Evil, in its essence, refuses to accept God as God and puts someone or
something else in his place. In the Bible, anything that goes against
God's moral will is presented as evil—starting with Adam and Eve's
first transgression in Eden. Their act was a blatant offense against God
and his righteousness, and it brought human *suffering* as the result. So

while suffering is clearly an effect of moral evil, suffering itself is not the same as moral evil.

⊛ INTERACT

⚔ Most people today understand evil as anything that harms others. The more harm done, the more evil the action.

Cornelius Plantinga named his book about sin after a line from the movie *Grand Canyon:* "Not the way it's supposed to be." Evil is exactly that—a fundamental and troubling departure from goodness. The Bible uses the word *evil* to describe anything that violates God's moral will. The first human evil occurred when Eve and Adam disobeyed God. From that original sin—a moral evil—came the consequence of suffering. Although suffering results from moral evil, it is distinguishable from it, just as an injury caused by drunken driving isn't synonymous with the offense.

Evil could be defined as "the refusal to accept the true God as God." True evil elevates itself or another to replace God. For this very reason, the Bible treats idolatry as the ultimate sin, since it worships as God what is *not* God. ⚔

1. How does the Bible's view of evil differ from the more popular understanding of evil as "anything that harms others"?

⚔ Some view evil as the absence of good.

The logic goes like this: There is no such thing as cold, only lower degrees of heat (or the complete lack of it). Darkness is not the opposite of light, but the absence of light. Death is not the opposite of life, but its privation. A cloth can exist without a hole, but that hole cannot exist without the cloth. Good can, did, and will exist without evil. But evil cannot exist without the good it opposes. A shadow is nothing but the obstruction of light—no light, no shadow....

More than merely the absence of good, evil is the cor-
ruption of good....

Perhaps we could better conceive of evil as a parasite
on God's good creation, since a parasite is something substantial. Without the living organism it uses as a host, the
parasite cannot exist. Likewise, cancer thrives on, con-
sumes, and ultimately kills healthy, living cells. As metal
does not need rust, but rust needs metal, so good doesn't
need evil, but evil needs good. ✗

2. Why is it important to understand that evil is more than
   merely the absence of good?

✗ Disobeying God, inseparable from the failure to trust
God, was the original evil. From that sin—a *moral* evil—
came the consequence of suffering. So suffering follows
evil as a caboose follows an engine. Scripture sometimes
refers to calamities and tragic events as evils. To distin-
guish these, we can call moral evil *primary* evil and suffering *secondary* evil....

Secondary evils point to primary evil, reminding us that
humanity, guilty of sin, deserves suffering. ✗

3. How does our sin contribute to the existence of suffering?

◉● EXPLORE FURTHER

(For more exploration, look over especially the **bold-text** sentences in
IGIG chapter 3, and then answer the questions below.)

4. How exactly would you define *evil*?

5. How would you define *suffering*?

6. Glance over *IGIG* chapter 3 and look for these quoted passages: Isaiah 5:20; Hebrews 5:14; Joshua 23:15; Romans 1:27. What information do they provide about God's view of evil and the causes of evil?

7. Look also at these passages quoted in chapter 3: Ephesians 2:7 and Jeremiah 32:38–42. What do they teach about God's grace and mercy toward us in the midst of an evil world?

8. In this chapter of *IGIG,* as you look over the bold-text statements, which one seems most important to you right now? Why?

⬤⬤⬤ INVESTIGATE DEEPER

(For more intensive study, read *IGIG* chapter 3.)

9. In your own words, how would you explain the distinction Randy makes between the "primary" evil of sin and the "secondary" evil of suffering?

10. Which stories or illustrations in *IGIG* chapter 3 did you find most valuable, and why?

11. Look up the following passages in your Bible, and record what they teach us about the tragic consequences of evil: Genesis 6:11–13; Isaiah 13:11; 24:4–6; 59:1–3.

What Are Some Possible Responses to the Problem of Evil and Suffering?
    (See also chapter 4 in *IGIG,* page 30.)

⊛ FOCUS IN

The irrational solution is to say that evil and suffering are illusions—that they don't really exist. The atheistic solution is to say that God doesn't exist. The more common way of addressing the problem of evil is to minimize one or more of the attributes of God, particularly his power, his knowledge, or his goodness. The Bible, however, consistently portrays God as infinite and limitless in all of his attributes.

To glorify and magnify God is not to make more of him than he is; that's impossible. Rather, it's to affirm his greatness, attempting to do justice to his infinite majesty, power, wisdom, love, etc., even though inevitably we'll fall short.

To address good and evil without gazing upon God is fruitless. Good flows from the life connected to God. Evil flows from the life alienated from God.

⊛ INTERACT

⨉ *How can we reconcile evil and suffering with a God who is all-good, all-powerful, and all-knowing?* I will present and comment briefly on six answers, returning later to develop several of them....

1. There is no evil and suffering....
2. There is no God....
3. God has limited goodness....
4. God has limited power....
5. God has limited knowledge....
6. God is all-good, all-powerful, and all-knowing; he hates evil and will ultimately judge evildoers, and remove evil and suffering after accomplishing a greater, eternal good.

How does your own worldview stack up against the real world around you? Does it credibly explain the way things are and offer persuasive reasons for believing in a hopeful future? Or do you need to revise or abandon it in order to embrace the biblical worldview because it better explains your condition and that of the world around you? ✠

1. How would you personally respond to the questions in the paragraph above?

✠ A friend wrestled with the problem of evil after a terrible accident. He concluded that we err whenever we speak of only two or three attributes of God in relation to the problem of evil. He meant that we must bring *all* of God's attributes to the table.

If we see God only in terms of his love, mercy, and compassion, we will not envision the true God, but only an idol of our own imagination—and that is precisely what we see in the airbrushed God of various modern solutions to the problem of evil. ✠

2. Why is it inadequate to "see God only in terms of his love, mercy, and compassion"? What other important aspects of his character do we need to understand?

✠ We must form our perspective from God's Word, not popular culture.

We live in an era when popular culture, despite its shallowness, has a far-reaching influence on the average person's worldview. This entertainment-driven and self-gratification-obsessed blend of pop psychology, pop philosophy, and pop theology has become its own worldview. Never have people needed to hear the biblical worldview

28   The Burning Question

more—and perhaps never have they been more culturally conditioned to dismiss it....

Studying about evil and suffering doesn't equal facing it, but the study and discussion can go a long way in preparing us for it. It will provide a reservoir of perspective from which we can draw. It will minimize disorientation and panic when we plunge into life's turbulence. This is why I encourage you to meditate on and discuss with others the themes of this book.

We shouldn't wait until suffering comes to start learning about how to face it any more than we should wait until we fall into the water to start learning how to scuba dive. ❖

3. You're to be commended for pursuing more understanding of God's perspective on this topic by working through this study guide! From your perspective, what would it mean to be adequately prepared for suffering? What would that look like in your own life?

❊❊ EXPLORE FURTHER

(For more exploration, review the **bold-text** sentences in *IGIG* chapter 4, and then answer the following questions.)

4. Mark these quoted passages: Isaiah 25:8; Deuteronomy 10:17; 32:3; 1 Chronicles 29:11. What do they show us about God's character and personality? And why is it important to understand these things as we search for answers about evil and suffering?

5. Look also at these scriptures in chapter 4: Luke 1:46; 3 John 11; Psalm 119:92. What additional insight do they provide about God, evil, or suffering?

6. In this chapter of *IGIG,* as you look over the bold-text statements, which one is the most significant for you right now, and why?

⊛●● INVESTIGATE DEEPER

(For more intensive study, read *IGIG* chapter 4.)

7. Look over the six worldviews Randy mentions in this chapter (pages 30–34). Setting aside the last one for now, which of the first five worldviews seems to have the most credibility?

8. What's the right heart and mind attitude to have toward God as we investigate the problem of evil and suffering?

9. Which stories or illustrations in *IGIG* chapter 4 did you find yourself most drawn to, and why?

A Closer Look at Central Issues in the Problem of Evil
   (See also chapter 5 in *IGIG,* page 40.)

⊛ FOCUS IN

Believers and unbelievers alike are horrified by the degree and extent of suffering in the world around us. Seeing and hearing about such vast affliction and anguish, we find it impossible to view it as an acceptable norm. This abhorrence of evil and suffering can help nudge unbelievers toward greater attentiveness to the Bible's promise of something better.

For the New Testament lets us know that our present sufferings ultimately serve our greater good. We're told, in fact, that this ultimate, eternal good will be so surpassingly wonderful that our present sufferings aren't even worth comparing to it.

In fact, the argument for the *greater good* may be the strongest biblical case for God permitting evil and suffering. Is it possible that we learn things through suffering that otherwise we might not understand so clearly? Can we trust the testimony of God's Word that in permitting evil he has good eternal purposes that are beyond our comprehension?

⊛ INTERACT

✣ As frequently expressed, the problem of evil assumes that an all-good, all-powerful, and all-knowing God cannot have good reasons for creating a universe in which evil and suffering exist. But shouldn't this assumption require some proof?

We may not understand why a good God would allow terrible suffering. But this merely establishes that if there is a God, we do not know everything he knows. Why should this surprise us?

Suppose we add only one premise to the argument that God is all-powerful, all-knowing, and all-loving, and yet evil exists: *God has a morally sufficient reason for permitting evil.* You may disagree with this premise, but it does *not* contradict the others....

To disprove the God of the Bible exists, someone must demonstrate there can be no moral justification for an all-good, all-powerful, and all-knowing God to allow evil. Has this been proven? No. This doesn't mean the question isn't valid, only that a question is not the same as a proof. ✣

1. What is your initial reaction to the statement, "God has a morally sufficient reason for permitting evil"? Do you tend to agree or disagree—and what are your reasons?

✖ Believers share common ground with unbelievers. We feel mutual horror at the reality, depth, and duration of human and animal suffering. We share a conviction that this kind of pain is terribly wrong and that it should be made right. In this way, evil and suffering serve as a bridge to the biblical account and its promise of redemption.

Consider two claims of Scripture: "Our present sufferings are not worth comparing with the glory that will be revealed in us" (Romans 8:18). "Our light and momentary troubles are achieving for us an eternal glory that far outweighs them all" (2 Corinthians 4:17)....

Paul insists that our sufferings will result in our greater good—God's people will be better off *eternally* because they suffer *temporarily.* From Paul's perspective, this trade-off will in eternity prove to be a great bargain....

Suffering reminds us to stop taking life for granted and to contemplate the larger picture. God intends that it draw our attention to life-and-death realities far greater than ourselves....

The dysfunction of the present is the exception, not the rule—a small fraction of our history. Evil, suffering, and death will end forever (see Revelation 21:4). May we learn now what Paul knew: our present sufferings are a brief but important part of a larger plan that one day will prove them all worthwhile. ✖

2. When we're experiencing suffering, why is it often hard for us to look beyond our pain toward eternity? What can help us have a stronger eternal perspective?

⚫ EXPLORE FURTHER

(For more exploration, review the **bold-text** sentences in *IGIG* chapter 5, and then answer the following questions.)

3. Find and mark these quoted passages: Romans 8:18 and
   2 Corinthians 4:17. According to these verses, what factor
   should we always remember as we evaluate our sufferings?

4. Look at Psalm 16:11 and Matthew 8:12, quoted in this
   chapter. What specifics about our future do they describe?

5. Find 1 Corinthians 15:32, quoted in this chapter. How
   does our future resurrection relate to our current existence
   and behavior?

6. In this chapter of *IGIG,* as you look over the bold-text
   statements, which one is most significant right now for
   your life, and why?

●●● **INVESTIGATE DEEPER**
(For more intensive study, read *IGIG* chapter 5.)
   7. What is the meaning of the term *theodicy*?

8. Which stories or illustrations in *IGIG* chapter 5 did you
   find yourself most drawn to, and why?

9. Look up 2 Corinthians 11:23–33 in your Bible. What specific hardships did the apostle Paul have to suffer in his life?

Tragic Choices

UNDERSTANDING EVIL: ITS ORIGINS, NATURE, AND CONSEQUENCES

(Links with section 2 in *If God Is Good,* pages 45–92.)

Evil's Entry into the Universe: A Rebellion of Angels
(See also chapter 6 in *IGIG,* page 47.)

❋ **FOCUS IN**

Scripture addresses *when* evil came into being, but not *how.* God has chosen to remain silent on the how, which may mean something significant. If evil is irrational, how can its point of origin be rationally explained? Perhaps God doesn't offer any explanation because evil defies explanation. It might make sense to an all-knowing God but no sense at all to us.

There are cultures throughout the world where people accept the reality of the supernatural, and they often encounter demonic activity openly as an oppressive, intimidating spiritual force. But in cultures like ours where supernatural reality is often ignored or overlooked, demons find it better to operate more stealthily. How astonished and terrified we would be if we could only see the emotional, mental, spiritual, and relational wreckage these evil spirits are causing all around us among otherwise "normal" people.

✺ INTERACT

✛ In cultures where everyone realizes there's a supernatural world, demons make themselves known as false gods to intimidate people, demanding worship and exacting retribution. In modern Western cultures where people routinely deny the supernatural, demons often accomplish their purposes more effectively by flying under the radar and working covertly. If we had eyes to see, we'd realize that all around us, fallen humans become the unwitting tools of evil spirits, harming themselves and others, and living wretched lives, sometimes quietly under the facade of social respectability. ✛

1. What is your understanding of the reality and danger of Satan and demons?

✛ It's misleading to say "God created Satan and demons." Rather, God created Lucifer and other righteous angels, who later chose to rebel against God, and in so doing *became* Satan and demons.

Evil entered the universe through Satan, then the fallen angels....

Satan and the demons dreamed of having authority over themselves and exalting themselves above God. They sinned by desiring to have more power than God appointed to them....

The Bible tells us about the *entry* of evil into the universe, but evil's ultimate *origin* remains a mystery....

Deuteronomy 29:29 seems to apply here: "The secret things belong to the LORD our God." ✛

2. Both fallen angels (demons) and fallen human beings were created by God, and both share the guilt of rebellion

against their Creator. Why is that rebellion such an evil thing in God's eyes?

⨳ God has good reasons for delaying his final judgment against Satan....

God has both the power and the right to destroy Satan and the demons *now*, which would demonstrate his justice. But he wants to display his other attributes as well, among them grace, mercy, and patience.

Every day that God delays his final judgment against Satan is one more day to extend his grace to a needy world. And it is one more day for his kindness in Christ to accomplish in this fallen world the work for which we will be praising him ten million years from now....

To embrace Jesus as our redeemer is to be delivered from considerable evil and suffering now, and eventually from *all* evil and suffering. Jesus liberates us and calls us to testify to others of his mercy and power to defeat evil and relieve suffering. ⨳

3. Think about what God has done through Jesus to overthrow and eventually extinguish the power of Satan and demons. How does this demonstrate God's mercy and love toward us?

● ● **EXPLORE FURTHER**
(For more exploration, review the **bold-text** sentences in *IGIG* chapter 6, and then respond below.)

4. What part do Satan and demons play in the problem of evil and suffering?

5. Look over the explanation of Mark 5:1–20 at the beginning of *IGIG* chapter 6. What does this passage show us about what Jesus wants to do, can do, and will do to demonic powers? How and why are these powers so harmful to people?

6. The following quoted passages in *IGIG* chapter 6 tell us something about what Satan (the devil) is like. Find and mark the passages, and summarize the important information they give us: John 8:44; Matthew 13:19; John 12:31; Revelation 12:9–10; Matthew 12:24; Revelation 12:4; 2 Corinthians 4:4; Ephesians 2:2; 6:12; 1 Peter 5:8; 2 Corinthians 11:14.

7. Look at these quoted scriptures and summarize the destiny of Satan and his forces: Genesis 3:14–15; Hebrews 2:14; 1 John 3:8; Colossians 2:15; Revelation 20:10; 12:12; 20:7–9; Jude 6.

8. In this chapter of *IGIG,* as you look over the bold-text statements, choose one that is the most significant for your life, and explain why.

●●● INVESTIGATE DEEPER
(For more intensive study, read *IGIG* chapter 6.)

9. Find Deuteronomy 29:29 in the chapter. What are the important implications of this passage as it relates to our understanding of God, evil, and suffering?

10. From what the Bible teaches, how would you explain the existence of Satan and demons?

11. Read the prophetic passages regarding the king of Babylon in Isaiah 14:12–15 and the king of Tyre in Ezekiel 28:11–19. These are often interpreted as references to Satan. What do you see in these passages that seems consistent with what you know to be true about Satan?

12. Which stories or illustrations in *IGIG* chapter 6 did you find yourself most drawn to, and why?

Humanity's Evil and the Suffering It Has Caused
(See also chapter 7 in *IGIG,* page 55.)

✴ FOCUS IN

Somehow, as the first human couple weighed their alternatives, evil entered their hearts. Adam and Eve rebelled, choosing to violate God's explicit command. They trusted a fallen creature's logic rather than their Creator's goodness, when he'd given them no reason to doubt him. They ate, the curse fell on them, their pain greatly increased, the Earth became a world of hurt, and they forfeited paradise.

God justly fulfilled his threat to Adam and Eve that the day they sinned, they died (see Genesis 2:17). How? They were separated from God immediately and consequently began to experience the protracted sentence of suffering that would eventually lead to their physical death (see Romans 6:23). However, God's punishment was measured in that he did not bring immediate physical death, which would have meant there could be no redemption or ongoing human history.

The history of the human race, in every culture and time, demonstrates the dire consequences of living life as we prefer rather than as God commands.

⊕ INTERACT

✠ At its root, evil violates God's nature and insults his supremacy. It rejects God and rebels against his authority. Therefore we cannot understand evil without understanding the nature of the one true God.

God's character provides the basis for moral standards: "Be holy because I, the LORD your God, am holy" (Leviticus 19:2)....

To sin is to exalt self and to depreciate the God who created us to live in loving relationship with him. ✠

1. How is humanity's sin an insult to God?

✠ The first humans, although created sinless, chose to rebel against God....

The Fall, the first human tragedy, became the mother of all subsequent ones. We should do nothing to minimize it or to pretend it mattered less than it did. Yet, the Fall did *not* end God's plan for humanity. God would ultimately use evil to accomplish the greater end of redemption in Christ....

Because the Fall really happened in history, God's Son had to enter history (incarnation), suffer and die in history (redemption), and rise from the grave in history (resurrection). ✠

2. In what ways do people today often minimize man's first fall into sin (through Adam and Eve's disobedience)? Does this historical fact have the preeminence it should have in the world? Why or why not?

⤜ The Christian worldview's account of evil and suffering
is uniquely and profoundly God-centered....

Everyone has a worldview, inconsistent and superficial
though it might be. Worldviews invite contemplation and
comparison. As I have compared the Christian worldview to
others, I have found it both comprehensive and satisfying. I
believe the greatest test of any worldview is how it deals
with the problem of evil and suffering. And Scripture's redemptive story passes that test with remarkable depth and
substance. ⤛

3. How would you describe your own worldview? What are
the major principles and perspectives that affect how you
view the world around you?

◉◉ EXPLORE FURTHER

(For more exploration, review the **bold-text** sentences in *IGIG* chapter 7,
and then respond to the following questions.)

4. Why does man's own sinfulness need to be brought into the
picture as we examine the problem of evil and suffering?

5. In *IGIG* chapter 7, find and mark the following quoted
passages, and summarize the insight and information they
provide regarding man's evil and suffering: Judges 21:25;
Romans 3:23; Genesis 3:16; 3:17.

6. Look also at the following quoted scriptures in this chapter,
and summarize their teaching about God's response to
humanity's evil and suffering: John 1:29; Hebrews 2:17;
Ephesians 1:9–11.

7. Also mark these quoted passages in chapter 7: Leviticus 19:2; Romans 3:23; Genesis 1:1; Isaiah 60:19. Taken together, how do they portray the "big picture" we need to keep in mind when we examine suffering and evil in our world?

8. In this chapter of *IGIG,* as you look over the bold-text statements, which one stands out to you, and why?

●●● INVESTIGATE DEEPER
(For more intensive study, read *IGIG* chapter 7.)

9. To what extent are human beings to blame for their own suffering?

10. In what important ways is the Christian worldview one that "sees evil for what it is," as Randy puts it (page 59)?

11. Which stories or illustrations in *IGIG* chapter 7 did you find most memorable, and why?

12. Look up in your Bible Romans 5:12–21; 1 Corinthians 15:22, 45; 1 Timothy 2:13–14. How do these passages affirm the historical reality of Adam and Eve?

Inherited Sin and Our Sin Nature
(See also chapter 8 in *IGIG,* page 62.)

✦ FOCUS IN

The *sin nature* refers to our fallen state that distrusts, dishonors, and rejects God.

The sin nature compels us to love ourselves. In our reckless pursuit of self-gratification, we impose upon ourselves gnawing emptiness rather than the joy and contentment that comes in loving God and others.

Though we naturally resist the biblical revelation about our sin natures, we find freedom when we recognize its reality.

To view evil accurately, we must see it above all as an outrageous offense against God.

We tend to minimize our sin because we fail to see its real object; because we don't see God and see how our sin hurts *him,* we don't see either the frequency or the gravity of our offenses. We imagine our sin has no effect on him.

We couldn't be more wrong.

✦ INTERACT

�֎ We grasp the horror of human evil only when we focus on God's standards and on the atonement necessary to satisfy them.

Anything that violates God's nature is evil. Sin is not merely a minor deviation from a negotiable standard. It is, in the eyes of a holy God and the holy angels who serve him, a despicable aberration from God's nature.

The clearest indication of our evil's depth is what it cost to redeem us. Some talk as if God's bighearted love for us is sufficient to save us. But the problem of how to reconcile evil people with a God who hates evil is the greatest problem of history. It calls for no less than the greatest solution ever devised, one so radical as to be nearly unthinkable, and to offend the sensibilities of countless people throughout history. ֎

1. What are some of the human violations of God's nature that seem to occur most commonly?

�֍ *Total spiritual inability* is a better description of the human condition....

    Scripture insists that all human beings are sinners, that sin touches every part of us, and that we cannot earn God's favor (see Isaiah 64:6; Romans 7:15; 8:8; Hebrews 11:6). God owes us nothing, while we owe him everything. We need God to reach down to us so that we may reach up to him....

    We remain helpless sinners with nothing to offer God that could gain us a right standing with him. ✗

2. Most of us have a noticeable inner resistance to the idea that we're really "helpless sinners with nothing to offer God that could gain us a right standing with him." If you sense that resistance, what forms does it take? What thoughts does it bring to mind?

✖ Inherited sin speaks of our moral condition resulting from the Fall....

    Various scriptures speak of or imply the doctrine of inherited sin (see Psalm 51:5; 58:3; Romans 5:12–19; 1 Corinthians 15:22).

    These passages tell us we are "sinful at birth" and "from birth...go astray," that "the many died by the trespass of one man," that "through the disobedience of the one man the many were made sinners," and that "in Adam all die."...

    Believing in the doctrine of inherited sin provides the ultimate equalizer. Embracing it leads to humility and grace, prompting us to care for the needy—individuals we might otherwise despise.

Ironically, wherever societies recognize the human capacity for evil, evil is restrained and goodness is exalted. Yet whenever people view themselves as basically good, the greatest evils take place. Denying the doctrine of inherited sin leads to elitism and oppression. Why? Partly because people who view themselves as good place no restrictions upon those in power. ⚔

3. How convinced are you that the doctrines of "total spiritual inability" and "inherited sin" are true? What factors have influenced your view on this?

⚔ The idea of inherited sin may seem unfair, but God is the proper Judge of fairness....

It never occurs to most of us that the book title *When Bad Things Happen to Good People* is based on a fundamental falsehood. What if, as the Bible teaches, no people are *truly* good? What if an evil deep within enslaves even the people we consider "good"?...

Bad things do not happen to good people. Why not? Because in this world truly good people do not exist. Although God created us in his image and we have great worth to him, the fact remains that we are fallen and corrupt, are under the Curse, and deserve Hell. ⚔

4. Why is it ultimately wrong for us to ever accuse God of unfairness?

⊛⦁ EXPLORE FURTHER

(For more exploration, review the **bold-text** sentences in *IGIG* chapter 8, and then answer the following questions.)

5. Do you believe human beings are basically good or basically bad? Or how would you describe your position on this?

6. Find the following quoted passages in this chapter, and then summarize their teaching about humanity's sinful nature: Jeremiah 17:9; Romans 3:10–18; 3:23; 1 John 1:8; Ephe-sians 2:3; 4:18.

7. Mark and restate in your own words what the following quoted scriptures show us regarding the truth and critical importance of the gospel: Ephesians 2:1; Matthew 5:48; James 2:10; John 3:18; Romans 4:3; Hebrews 11:6; John 16:9; 1 John 5:10.

8. Also mark these quoted passages, and then summarize their teaching about humanity's future judgment and/or salvation: Revelation 20:12; Romans 2:6; Colossians 3:25; Romans 5:19; 1 Corinthians 15:22.

9. In this chapter of *IGIG,* as you look over the bold-text statements, which one is most important to you, and why?

◉ ◉ ● INVESTIGATE DEEPER
(For more intensive study, read *IGIG* chapter 8.)

10. Does Scripture teach that human beings are basically good or basically bad?

11. What is the doctrine of "total depravity," and why is "total spiritual inability" a better name for it?

12. Why is this doctrine of "total depravity" or "total spiritual inability" so important for us to grasp?

13. What is the doctrine of "inherited sin," and why do we need to understand and accept it?

14. Which stories or illustrations in *IGIG* chapter 8 did you find yourself most drawn to, and why?

15. Find the following passages in your Bible: Romans 2:15; 1 Corinthians 4:4; 8:7; 1 Timothy 4:2; Titus 1:15. What do they teach us about our conscience?

16. Look up the following passages in your Bible, and summarize what they say about the doctrine of inherited sin: Psalm 51:5; 58:3; Romans 5:12–19; 1 Corinthians 15:22.

A Deeper Consideration of What Our Sin Nature Does and Doesn't Mean
   (See also chapter 9 in *IGIG,* page 74.)

❋ FOCUS IN

Apart from Christ, I am Osama bin Laden. I am Hitler. Only by the virtue of Christ can I stand forgiven before a holy God. This isn't hyperbole; it's biblical truth. Unless we come to grips with the fact that we're of precisely the same stock as history's most murderous oppressors, we'll never get over thinking that we deserve better. Evil done to us will offend us, and having to suffer will outrage us. We'll never appreciate Christ's grace so long as we hold on to the proud illusion that we're better than we are. We flatter ourselves when we look at evil acts and say, "I would *never* do that." Given our evil natures and a change in background, resources, and opportunities, we *would*.

⊛ INTERACT

✖ Despite our righteous standing in Christ, believers remain prone to sin.

Christians have received the resources in Christ to please him, to turn from sin, and to live holy and righteous lives (see Titus 2:11–12). God has given to us in Christ and his indwelling Spirit the ability not to sin. Some, however, take our righteous standing in Christ to mean we're no longer able to sin. Scripture clearly contradicts this (see James 3:2; 1 John 1:8–10)....

Only one who is deeply aware of his evil tendencies will humbly take the necessary steps to guard his heart from sin.

Jesus said, "The truth will set you free" (John 8:32). I've found tremendous freedom in knowing that I am a great sinner. It helps deliver me from pretending I'm better than I am. It makes me more honest before God and others, and hopefully more truly humble (as opposed to merely *appearing* to be humble as a prideful strategy). ✖

1. What has God done to humble you and make you more deeply aware of your own sinful tendencies?

✖ The greater our grasp of our sin and alienation from God, the greater our grasp of God's grace....

Grace isn't about God lowering his standards. It's about God fulfilling those standards through the substitutionary suffering of Jesus Christ. Grace never ignores or violates truth. Grace gave what truth demanded: the ultimate sacrifice for our wickedness.

God's grace is greater than my sin. But my ability to measure the greatness of his grace depends upon my willingness, in brokenness before him, to recognize the greatness of my sin. "God opposes the proud but gives grace to the humble" (1 Peter 5:5). The proud deny their evil; the humble confess it.

A profound awareness of my evil should move my heart to praise God for the wonders of his grace. ⊀

2. How would you express in your own words the "wonders" of God's grace to you?

⊁ Having sin natures doesn't mean we are as evil as we could possibly be or that all people do equal amounts of evil....

Despite our bondage to sin and our inability to earn God's favor, human beings can make some good choices....

If humanity lacked all goodness, the human race could not survive.

Drivers would disobey every traffic signal, all police would become utterly corrupt, every pedestrian would be robbed, every house plundered. Murder, rape, and other cruel acts would reign. No driver would nod to let a man cross the street, except to run him down. The poor and disabled would face extinction. Just laws would not exist. All parents would abandon their children to the streets....

We should be profoundly grateful for God's restraint of evil, his delay of judgment, and his gift of goodness in this fallen world. ⊀

3. Despite the presence of evil and suffering in this world, what are some of the *good* things that you are most grateful for?

�֎ Ever since Adam blamed Eve for persuading him to eat the forbidden fruit, and Eve blamed the serpent for getting her to eat it, impugning others has become the normal human practice (see Genesis 3:12–13). Accusing another allows us to justify our own sin.

Our culture of blame, exemplified by frivolous lawsuits, goes hand in hand with a sense of entitlement. We think we deserve the best and are offended when we don't get it. We feel outraged at wrongs done to us—whether real or imagined....

Instead of bemoaning our own predicaments, how often do we look at the world, with all its evil and suffering, and say to God, "Forgive me for my part in the world's sin"?

It's easy to blame God for not doing all he can to stop evil and suffering. But consider that he has graciously allowed the world to continue while postponing final judgment. Consider that he has put us in this world with a mission that includes resisting evil and relieving suffering. Consider that he has entrusted us with vast resources to carry out that mission.

We just might want to ask if we, and not God, are to blame. ✗

4. Randy mentions that Christians in this world have "a mission that includes resisting evil and relieving suffering." Practically speaking, what do you think that mission means for you?

⦿ ● EXPLORE FURTHER

(For more exploration, review the **bold-text** sentences in *IGIG* chapter 9, and then respond to the questions below.)

5. Who would you say was the worst person in human history? How would you compare that person's evil with the evil you see in yourself and in your friends and family?

6. Look for the following quoted passages in this chapter, and identify and record the ways in which any of them relate personally to you and to the sin in your own life: James 4:17; Proverbs 24:11–12; Jeremiah 4:22; James 3:2; 1 Timothy 1:15; 1 Peter 5:5; Ecclesiastes 7:20.

7. In this chapter of *IGIG,* as you look over the bold-text statements, which one has the most significance right now, and why?

⦿ ● ● INVESTIGATE DEEPER

(For more intensive study, read *IGIG* chapter 9.)

8. Why is it so important for us to take our own measure of responsibility for evil and suffering? What happens when we don't?

9. Which stories or illustrations in *IGIG* chapter 9 did you find yourself most drawn to, and why?

Natural Disasters: Creation Under the Curse of Human Evil
   (See also chapter 10 in *IGIG*, page 84.)

◉ FOCUS IN

Earthquakes and tsunamis are not moral agents and therefore cannot be morally evil. A tidal wave isn't malicious—water cannot have malice any more than it can have kindness.

The best answer to the question "Why would God create a world with natural disasters?" is that *he didn't.* Many experts believe the world's atmosphere originally acted like an umbrella, protecting its inhabitants from harm. But now the umbrella has holes in it, sometimes protecting us, sometimes not. While some blame God for death and disaster, Scripture blames human evil for the cataclysmic Fall and consequent distortion of a once-perfect world (see Romans 8:18–22).

For survivors of a natural disaster, the experience often brings about a profound recognition that this present world—so frightfully disfigured and broken and menacing—can never truly be the place of security and comfort we deeply long for.

◉ INTERACT

✚ Many people blame God for natural disasters…. But what if the Architect and Builder crafted a beautiful and perfect home for Earth's inhabitants, who despite his warnings carelessly cracked its foundation, punched holes in the walls, and trashed the house? Why blame the builder when the occupants took a sledgehammer to their own home?…

Natural disasters become most disastrous when they take human life—but they never did so until after humans committed moral evil against God.

God placed a curse on the earth due to Adam's sin (see Genesis 3:17)…. Paul says that "the creation was subjected to frustration" by God's curse, until that day when "the creation itself will be liberated from its bondage to decay" (Romans 8:20–21). The next verse says, "The whole creation has been groaning as in the pains of childbirth." Earthquakes, volcanoes, and tsunamis reflect the frustration, bondage, and decay of an earth groaning under sin's curse....

People who have survived disasters often say they understand on a far deeper level the biblical truth that this world *as it now is*—under the Curse—is not our home. ⚔

1. Why is it important and helpful for us to realize that "this world *as it now is*...is not our home"?

⚔ Disasters can initiate self-examination...bring out the best in people...lead to spiritual transformation....

When we face a natural disaster, disease, or even a financial hardship, we should ask God, "What are you trying to tell us?"

A world without personal tragedy or natural disasters would produce no heroes.

Life brings more personal disasters than national or global ones—and God can bring good out of any of them. ⚔

2. What are some examples of how natural disasters can bring out the best in people?

⬤● EXPLORE FURTHER

(For more exploration, review the **bold-text** sentences in *IGIG* chapter 10, and then answer the following questions.)

3. What causes natural disasters? To what extent do you think human beings are to blame?

4. Glance over chapter 10, look for the following quoted passages, and restate in your own words what they show us

about God's control over nature's forces (including natural disasters): Psalm 147:18; Job 37:13; Numbers 11:1; Matthew 5:45; Amos 4:6–7, 9; Isaiah 45:7; Amos 3:6.

5. Look at the quoted verses from Job 1. What does the beginning of Job's story reveal about both God's and Satan's involvement in the disasters that struck Job?

6. In this chapter of *IGIG,* as you look over the bold-text statements, which one is most significant right now in your life, and why?

● ● ● INVESTIGATE DEEPER
(For more intensive study, read *IGIG* chapter 10.)

7. In your own words, how would you explain God's sovereign control over nature—including natural disasters?

8. Which stories or illustrations in *IGIG* chapter 10 seemed especially meaningful, and why?

9. Look up in your Bible and summarize in your own words the teaching of Romans 8:19–22 regarding the effect of humanity's sin upon the natural world around us, and why this is important to comprehend.

PART 2

Our Search for Solutions

(Links with sections 3–5 in If God Is Good, *pages 93–220)*

2-A

Alternative Answers

PROBLEMS FOR NON-THEISTS: MORAL STANDARDS, GOODNESS, AND EXTREME EVIL

(Links with section 3 in *If God Is Good,* pages 93–138.)

When a "Christian" Loses His Faith
(See also chapter 11 in *IGIG,* page 95.)

❋ FOCUS IN

A struggle with this issue might not cause us to make a clean break with our faith, but it will still typically weaken it. This seems especially true in the academic setting, where Christian students find themselves bombarded by forceful arguments against biblical faith from those who often emphasize the enormity of evil and suffering. Believing students find little defense against such an onslaught in the cheerful platitudes and simplified hero-tales they learned in Sunday school.

We all trust *something.* When we abandon trust in God's revelation, we replace it with trust in our own feelings, opinions, and preferences, or those of our friends and teachers—all of which can drift with popular culture, including academic culture.

❋ INTERACT

❧ In light of the great number of young people who reject their faith as college students or young adults, we need to ask ourselves two questions: What are we doing to help nominally Christian young people come to a true faith in Christ? And what are we doing to help youthful, genuine Christians go deeper in exploring Scripture, learning sound theology, and developing a truly Christian worldview, not a superficial one?...

Christian families, churches, and schools...need to carefully address the problem of evil.

Even Christians who do not outright reject their faith may quietly lose confidence and commitment because of their struggle with this issue. Christian students in every university, including Christian ones, face frequent, impassioned arguments against biblical teachings, whether from professors, fellow students, or textbooks. Most Christian students have seldom personally faced the problem of evil and suffering, and in most cases are inadequately prepared to deal with it. Knowing a few Bible stories proves insufficient when facing an issue of the magnitude of evil and suffering....

We should not allow culture or schools to lead the way in shaping our worldview, or our children's. ✕

1. If you're a parent (or hope to be someday), what are a few of the most important things you could do to help your children (and grandchildren) have a realistic and biblical understanding of evil and suffering?

✕ Isn't it remarkable that from Sudan to China to Cambodia to El Salvador, faith in God grows deepest in places where evil and suffering have been greatest?...

While Western atheists turn from belief in God because a tsunami in another part of the world caused great suffering, many brokenhearted survivors of that same tsunami found faith in God. This is one of the great paradoxes of suffering. Those who don't suffer much think suffering should keep people from God, while many who suffer a great deal turn *to* God, not *from* him....

You won't find the strongest Christian churches in the world in affluent America or Europe, where the problem of evil has the most traction. In Sudan, Christians are severely persecuted, raped, tortured, and sold into slavery. Yet many have a vibrant faith in Christ. People living in Garbage Village in Cairo make up one of the largest churches in Egypt. Hundreds of thousands of India's poor are turning to Christ. Why? Because the caste system and fatalism of Hinduism give them no answers. So they turn to a personal God who loves them and understands suffering. I have interviewed numbers of people who take comfort in knowing that this life is the closest they will ever come to Hell. ✠

2. What do you think Christians in the West can learn from persecuted Christians in other countries?

◦◦ EXPLORE FURTHER

(For more exploration, review the **bold-text** sentences in *IGIG* chapter 11, and then answer the following questions.)

3. Consider the story of Bart Ehrman. How would you summarize what happened to him?

4. Look at the quotation from Habakkuk 3:17–19 in chapter 11. What are the most significant contrasts you see between Habakkuk's response to God and that of the "Christian"-turned-atheist Bart Ehrman?

5. Look at God's words to Job in Job 40:2 and 41:11, quoted near the end of chapter 11. How are they also appropriate as God's words to Bart Ehrman? (And perhaps to you?)

6. In this chapter of *IGIG,* as you look over the bold-text statements, which one is most important to you, and why?

⊚ ⊛ ● INVESTIGATE DEEPER

(For more intensive study, read *IGIG* chapter 11.)

7. To what extent do you feel you can identify with Bart Ehrman, and why?

8. Although an atheist, Bart Ehrman cited the book of Ecclesiastes as reflecting his own view of suffering. Glance over the book of Ecclesiastes; how do you see it contradicting Ehrman's atheism? What does Ecclesiastes teach us about God?

9. In what ways does Bart Ehrman's story challenge you?

Non-Theistic Worldviews Lack a Substantial Basis for Condemning Evil

(See also chapter 12 in *IGIG,* page 108.)

⊛ FOCUS IN

I've talked with individuals whose ethics have evolved over time, who now believe that any consensual sex between adults is moral. Adultery is consensual sex. So is it moral? Well, yes, some convince themselves, so long as they commit adultery with a person they genuinely love. But how moral is this same adultery in the eyes of the betrayed spouse?

Choosing moral behaviors because they make you *feel* happy can make sense in a way…but what if it makes you feel happy to torture animals or kill Jews or steal from your employer?

Such hopeless subjectivity is no moral framework at all. Apart from a divine Creator who gives us a clear picture (in Scripture especially, but also in our conscience) of the moral conduct he expects from human beings, it's impossible for a person's moral values to ever be anything more than his or her personal opinions, totally lacking in authority for anyone else.

⊛ INTERACT

✖ It's difficult to argue the problem of evil when your worldview provides no basis for believing in evil….

I've read many atheists; typically, they present long lists of things that *they* call evil. But this poses a problem for them. In calling these things evil, [they try] to hold God accountable to moral standards that can exist *only if there is a God.…* If God does not exist, then there can be no ultimate right or wrong and no objective standards of goodness or evil beyond personal opinion or the majority votes of human cultures….

The Christian worldview's shaping influence on the Western world, to which most atheists strenuously object, is *exactly* what creates the moral tension needed to reveal evil and suffering as a moral problem….

If there is no God who created us for an eternal purpose, and no God who will judge us; if there is no God who has revealed his standards and no God who informs our consciences—then surely any morality we forge on our own will ultimately amount to a mirror image of our own subjective opinions that will change with the times….

We have only one basis for good moral judgments: the existence of objective standards based on unchanging reference points outside ourselves. Personal opinion falls far short. After all, Nazis and rapists have their opinions too. ✖

1. Why is it true that without God we can have no ultimate and absolute standards of goodness or evil?

That God has planted in all his image-bearers an ability to recognize good and evil in their consciences (see Romans 2:15) accounts for why people who do not believe Scripture can nonetheless feel guilty when they do wrong and feel good when they do right.

Even those who reject the claims of the Christian worldview should acknowledge that it does in fact offer a moral foundation upon which to discern good and evil. And they should ask themselves whether, without realizing it, they sometimes borrow from the Christian worldview because their own worldview cannot provide a foundation on which to judge good and evil.

2. What are some reasons we should be especially grateful that God created us with a conscience?

EXPLORE FURTHER

(For more exploration, review the **bold-text** sentences in *IGIG* chapter 12, and then respond below.)

3. In your observations, what basis for morality is given by people who don't believe in God?

4. How would you explain the true and correct basis for human morality?

5. In this chapter of *IGIG,* as you look over the bold-text statements, which one seems most significant right now, and why?

●●● **INVESTIGATE DEEPER**
(For more intensive study, read *IGIG* chapter 12.)

6. Do you agree or disagree that non-theistic worldviews have no substantial basis for condemning evil? Why?

7. What is most true about God that qualifies him as the only basis for human morality?

8. Which stories or illustrations in *IGIG* chapter 12 did you find yourself most drawn to, and why?

The Unbeliever's Problem of Goodness
    (See also chapter 13 in *IGIG,* page 119.)

● **FOCUS IN**

From a non-theistic viewpoint, what is evil? Isn't it just nature at work? In a strictly natural, physical world, shouldn't everything be neither good nor evil? Good and evil imply an "ought" and an "ought not" that nature is incapable of producing.

We have no logical reason to take good for granted; its existence demands an explanation. Why would we expect to find any goodness in a world that came about through blind force, time, and chance?

The atheist who points out the horrors of evil unwittingly testifies to good as the norm. When we speak of children dying, we acknowledge they usually don't. When a natural disaster hits, 99 percent of the world remains untouched. Though fallen, nature still contains more beauty than ugliness.

● INTERACT

�֍ While atheists routinely speak of the problem of evil, they usually don't raise the problem of goodness. But if evil provides evidence against God, then shouldn't goodness count as evidence for him?...

We have no logical reason to take good for granted; its existence demands an explanation.

Much of the good of this world, such as the beauty of a flower or the grandeur of a waterfall or the joy of an otter at play, serves no more practical purpose than great art. It does, however, serve a high purpose of filling us with delight, wonder, and gratitude....

That we don't question good's existence affirms we consider good the norm and evil the exception.

Don't evil and suffering grab our attention precisely because they are *not* the norm in our lives?...

Granted, in certain lives and times, suffering becomes the norm. Yet even then sufferers often retain a remarkable capacity for laughter and can find pleasure in flowers, a movie, a pet, or a friend. ✦

1. What are the strongest evidences of goodness that you see in your life and surroundings at this present time? In what ways do you recognize this goodness as being from God?

✖ The Christian worldview explains goodness as rooted in God, revealed by God and rewarded by him. It gives reason for optimism to those who embrace it....

Without God, the world would be amoral, with no objective goodness or evil....

Where does goodness come from? How could it come from nothing? Why would people have such a strong sense of right and wrong? Why would the powerful sometimes sacrifice their lives to save the weak, handicapped, and dying?

Evolution can explain greed, selfishness, insensitivity, survival-preoccupation, and even a certain amount of ruthlessness; but does anything in the blind evolutionary process explain demonstrating kindness, putting other people first, and even risking your life to help a stranger?...

Suppose we believe in a Creator who made people in his image, fashioning them to make effectual choices. Suppose those people chose sin, condemning themselves to live under death and curse, but that God still blessed them with his providence and common grace. In that case, wouldn't we expect the world to look as it does, with much goodness and evil coexisting? I think the answer is yes. ⚔

2. If you had to put a number on it, what percentage of all that exists in our world today would you say is *good,* what percentage would you say is *evil,* and what percentage (if any) would you say is mixed or neither?

⚔ Our desire to live proves that good is greater than evil and that most suffering can be tolerated....

If the quantity and intensity of evil and suffering in the world is so intolerable, why don't more people commit suicide, or at least seriously consider it? Could it be that the good they see in this world gives them hope for a better future? ⚔

3. How strong is your own will to live—to survive and endure—despite hardships and suffering? How would you describe your own "hope for a better future"?

⊛ ⊛ EXPLORE FURTHER
(For more exploration, review the **bold-text** sentences in *IGIG* chapter 13, and then answer the following questions.)

4. Have you ever wondered why there is good as well as evil in this world? What's your best answer to that question?

5. How does the existence of good in this world point to God?

6. In this chapter of *IGIG,* as you look over the bold-text statements, which one is most relevant to you, and why?

⊛ ⊛ ● INVESTIGATE DEEPER
(For more intensive study, read *IGIG* chapter 13.)

7. Give some biblical reasons why good exists, even in a fallen world.

8. Why is it impossible for good to exist without God?

9. Which stories or illustrations in *IGIG* chapter 13 stood out to you, and why?

The Unbeliever's Problem of Extreme Evil
  (See also chapter 14 in *IGIG,* page 131.)

● FOCUS IN

The atheistic worldview simply cannot account for superhuman evil. Death, yes; suffering, yes. But calculated, relentless, exhausting brutality toward the weak and innocent? The death camps? The Nazi doctors? The Killing Fields?

Why commit evil just for evil's sake, or why take pleasure in inflicting suffering? All pragmatic, naturalistic, and evolutionary explanations of such evil prove inadequate.

The Bible, on the other hand, speaks of an unseen realm full of powerful spirit beings that project their cruel and malignant thoughts and wills on humans. These beings, far more powerful than human beings, also exceed humans in their evil. These malevolent beings push us to expand our evil beyond the boundaries of what could be expected even of fallen humans.

No naturalistic worldview can explain extreme evil. Since non-theists believe in nothing outside of the visible realm, they must explain such evils on the basis of human perversity alone.

● INTERACT

✖ The problem of extreme evil...[is]...the most frequently cited argument against God, and many consider it the most devastating.

Surprisingly, however, upon closer examination, extreme evil may actually be seen as evidence *for* God's existence, not against it....

The Christian worldview explains the existence of extreme evil far better than atheism does....

Satan and demons provide the most rational explanation for unnatural evil....

Jesus gave us the answer when he said of Satan, "He was a murderer from the beginning" (John 8:44). ✖

1. When we think of the most horrifying evils that have existed in this world, why is it reasonable to assume the influence of Satan and demons?

✖ Extreme evil can wake us up to the reality of both good and evil, testifying to the invisible realities of God and Satan.

   Unbelievers and believers both call certain things utterly evil, including child abuse. Some will cite such evil as evidence against God. But others will see things for what they are and come face to face with the supernatural. When evil grows awful enough, the unbeliever may abandon the sinking ship of moral relativism and its conviction that absolute evil doesn't exist.

   Because the Christian worldview offers a well-grounded explanation for both human and superhuman evil, and a solid basis for moral outrage, those who find themselves morally outraged owe themselves a careful look at it. ✖

2. What should our response be to the extreme evil in this world that derives from satanic and demonic influence? How should our awareness affect our daily actions and attitudes?

◉◉ **EXPLORE FURTHER**

(For more exploration, review the **bold-text** sentences in *IGIG* chapter 14, and then answer the following questions.)

3. What would you say are some of the worst manifestations of evil this world has ever seen?

4. What do you think drives people to such heinous acts?

5. In this chapter of *IGIG,* as you look over the bold-text statements, which one seems most significant to you, and why?

⊛ ◉ ● INVESTIGATE DEEPER
(For more intensive study, read *IGIG* chapter 14.)

6. In what ways does the Christian worldview provide a better explanation for the existence of extreme evil than atheism does?

7. Is it true that God can use even the worst forms of evil for his own good purposes? Why or why not?

8. Which stories or illustrations in *IGIG* chapter 14 were most compelling, and why?

PROPOSED SOLUTIONS TO THE PROBLEM OF EVIL AND SUFFERING: LIMITING GOD'S ATTRIBUTES

(Links with section 4 in *If God Is Good,* pages 139–85.)

Is God's Limited Power *a Solution?*
(See also chapter 15 in *IGIG,* page 141.)

⊛ FOCUS IN
If God lacks power, his good intentions are inadequate. You probably already have friends who can't control the universe. Do you really need another one, named "God"?

Those who believe in a God of limited power might respond, "It isn't that God can't do anything, just that he can't do everything." But what *can* he do? If God is doing the best he can, then he doesn't *permit* evil and suffering, but is *overtaken* by them—since he can't stop them. Why frustrate God with prayers he can't answer, since if he could, he already would have?

Limiting God may appear to get him off the hook for life's difficulties. It might make us feel warmer toward him. But this is a god of man's invention, not the God revealed in Scripture.

⊛ INTERACT

�֎ It has become theologically trendy to speak of God's weakness, powerlessness, and vulnerability. Writers argue that Jesus didn't restrain himself from exercising power to liberate himself from his captors and the Cross—they believe he had no power to do so....

Scripture speaks of Christ's "incomparably great power" and "mighty strength" that made possible his resurrection. Today he sits at God's right hand, "far above all rule and authority, power and dominion, and every title that can be given, not only in the present age but also in the one to come. And God placed all things under his feet and appointed him to be head over everything" (Ephesians 1:19–21)....

Scripture emphatically reveals God as all-powerful....

"I am God, and there is no other; I am God, and there is none like me. I make known the end from the beginning, from ancient times, what is still to come. I say: My purpose will stand, and I will do all that I please.... What I have said, that will I bring about; what I have planned, that will I do" (Isaiah 46:9–11).

God is "the LORD strong and mighty, the LORD mighty in battle" (Psalm 24:8). The rhetorical question "Is anything too hard for the LORD?" implies a "no" answer (see Genesis 18:14; Jeremiah 32:27).

Gabriel says to Mary, "Nothing is impossible with God" (Luke 1:37). Jesus says, "With God all things are possible" (Matthew 19:26). ⚔

1. Why is it so important for us to recognize that God's power has no limits?

⚔ God's omnipotence and love are not in conflict. Jeremiah 32:17–19 affirms God's love in the midst of a passage not minimizing his power but exalting it: "Ah, Sovereign LORD, you have made the heavens and the earth by your great power and outstretched arm. *Nothing is too hard for you. You show love to thousands....* O great and powerful God, whose name is the LORD Almighty, great are your purposes and mighty are your deeds." ⚔

2. Why is the idea of God being limited in power an inadequate explanation for why evil and suffering exist in this world?

◦ ● EXPLORE FURTHER

(For more exploration, review the **bold-text** sentences in *IGIG* chapter 15, and then respond to the questions below.)

3. What limits do people sometimes think there are to God's power?

4. In this chapter, find and mark the following quoted passages about God's power, then summarize what they teach us: Isaiah 46:9–11; Psalm 24:8; Luke 1:37; Matthew 19:26; 2 Corinthians 6:18; Ephesians 3:20; 1:19–21.

5. Look also at these quoted scriptures in this chapter: Psalm 103:13; Isaiah 49:15–16; Jeremiah 32:17–19. How do they show God's power and compassion working together?

6. What most convinces you that God is unlimited in his power?

7. In this chapter of *IGIG,* as you look over the bold-text statements, which one is most important and has the most significance for your life, and why?

◈ ◉ ● INVESTIGATE DEEPER
(For more intensive study, read *IGIG* chapter 15.)

8. Explain as fully as you can why it's impossible for God's limited power to be a solution to the problem of evil and suffering.

9. Which stories or illustrations in *IGIG* chapter 15 did you find yourself most drawn to, and why?

10. Look up in your Bible 2 Timothy 2:13 and Hebrews 6:18; what additional insight do they give us about God's power?

11. In respect to God's power, what can you now praise and worship him for?

Is God's **Limited Knowledge** *a Solution?*
(See also chapter 16 in *IGIG,* page 146.)

❋ FOCUS IN

A loving God took a calculated risk, open theists suggest, but had he known the horrible things that would occur—the rapes and killings and tortures and abuse—he might never have created this world as he did. Hence, proponents of open theism argue, God cannot be held responsible for his creatures' evil since he couldn't foresee it.

Open theists suppose we should find comfort in believing God hasn't ordained our suffering from eternity past. I find it easier to trust a God who has known all along and planned how he'll use the tragedy for his glory and our good, than one who just found out about it but chose not to stop it anyway.

Open theism is not only biblically wrong; it's a shallow answer to the problem of evil.

❋ INTERACT

➤ Open theists believe that God does not and cannot know in advance the future choices that his free creatures will make....

Open theism has become surprisingly influential—and its popularity continues to rise....

Open theism stands in contrast to the biblical and historical teaching that God knows absolutely everything.

God is *"perfect in knowledge"* (Job 37:16). He *"knows everything"* (1 John 3:20). "He determines the number of the stars and calls them each by name" (Psalm 147:4). That's countless trillions of stars, each named by God.

Jesus says, "Your Father knows what you need before you ask him," and, "Even the very hairs of your head are all numbered" (Matthew 6:8; 10:30). Even of plentiful sparrows, he says, "Not one of them is forgotten by God" (Luke 12:6)....

David says, "O LORD, you have searched me and known me! You know when I sit down and when I rise up; you discern my thoughts from afar.... *Even before a word is on my tongue,* lo, O LORD, you know it altogether" (Psalm 139:1–2, 4, ESV). From eternity past, God knew everything that will happen on every day of our lives: "Your eyes saw my unformed substance; in your book were written, every one of them, the days that were formed for me, when as yet there was none of them" (Psalm 139:16, ESV). God knows all the choices, free or not, we will ever make and all the consequences they will ever produce....

The charge that they don't really believe in God's omniscience offends open theists. Nevertheless, Christians throughout church history have believed that God's omniscience encompasses *all* knowledge—past, present, *and* future. ❖

1. Describe in your own words what it means that God is omniscient (all-knowing).

❖ God knows everything, including every contingency, and he knows what is ultimately best in ways we cannot. God can see ultimate purposes and plans that we can't. He can know it is better for someone to die now rather than later: "The righteous perish, and no one ponders it in his heart; devout men are taken away, and no one understands that the righteous are taken away to be spared from evil" (Isaiah 57:1).

We have no way of knowing, for instance, whether a disability might be used to cultivate personal qualities that would more profoundly honor God and bring the person greater eternal reward in Heaven.

Because God knows all things in the past, present, *and*

future, God is uniquely qualified to know when to ordain or permit evil and suffering and when not to.

2. Why is it so important for us to recognize that God's knowledge has no limits?

God, because of his comprehensive knowledge of the future, can bring eternal value out of evil and suffering.

God saw what would happen in a world of human beings, all able to choose. He saw the horrors that would come with the Fall and millennia of evil and suffering. But he also saw, from the very beginning, exactly how the ultimate good of manifesting his love and revealing the wonders of his grace would bring an eternal richness to the universe. He does not *hope* this to be the case. He *knows* this to be the case.

3. Were you familiar with open theism before reading this chapter? Do you agree with Randy that the idea of God being limited in knowledge is both unbiblical and an inadequate explanation for why evil and suffering exist in this world? Why or why not?

EXPLORE FURTHER

(For more exploration, review the **bold-text** sentences in *IGIG* chapter 16, and then respond below.)

4. What limits do people sometimes think there are to what God knows about the past, present, or future?

5. In this chapter, find and mark the following quoted passages about God's perfect (and timeless) knowledge and understanding, then summarize what they teach us: Job

37:16; 1 John 3:20; Psalm 147:4; Matthew 6:8; 10:30; Luke 12:6; Psalm 139:1–2, 4, 16; Isaiah 46:9–10.

6. Look also at these quoted scriptures in this chapter: Malachi 3:6; James 1:17; Hebrews 13:8. How do they affirm that God is unchanging?

7. What most convinces you that God is unlimited in what he knows?

8. In this chapter of *IGIG,* as you look over the bold-text statements, which one is most significant to you right now, and why?

⊚ ◉ ● INVESTIGATE DEEPER

(For more intensive study, read *IGIG* chapter 16.)

9. Explain as fully as you can why it's impossible for God's limited knowledge to be a solution to the problem of evil and suffering.

10. Which stories or illustrations in *IGIG* chapter 16 seemed most important, and why?

11. In respect to God's perfect knowledge, what would you like to praise and worship him for now?

Is God's Limited Goodness *a Solution?*
(See also chapter 17 in *IGIG,* page 163.)

◉ FOCUS IN

A good man doesn't knowingly allow his neighbor to beat his child. If he had all power, he would not only stop the man from beating the child, he wouldn't allow him to begin beating the child in the first place. Such an appraisal is completely apt regarding humans.

But we err in judging God by our standards.

We can envision a dog recognizing his master as good when he feeds and walks him, but questioning his owner's goodness when he doesn't let him have a Hershey's bar. He might even write a book or go on the lecture circuit telling everyone why his master isn't good.

The existence of evil does not contradict God's goodness, since God can ultimately use evil to bring about a greater good.

◉ INTERACT

⚔ God is the Greatest Good and is the source of all lesser goods: "Every good and perfect gift is from above, coming down from the Father" (James 1:17)....

God manifests his goodness to all people.

God does not restrict his goodness to believers only. He is good to all his creatures: "The LORD is good to all; he has compassion on all he has made" (Psalm 145:9)....

God grants his goodness to humanity at large, manifested in both nature and culture, in such good things as animals, forests, rivers, music, art, and sports.

God's goodness is absolute; there is no evil in him. ⚔

1. What is the greatest evidence to you that God's goodness is absolute?

✖ The existence of evil does not contradict God's goodness, since God can ultimately use evil to bring about a greater good....

To say that God is good is *not* to say God will always *appear* to be good, or that when he is good we will always like him for it....

God's acts of goodness may appear harsh or even cruel....

Hardship often cultivates Christlikeness in us and prepares us for greatness. Sheer kindness might keep us from the hardship that true love doesn't—especially all-knowing love that clearly sees the final result.

Some parents force their children to stay home most nights, do chores, study, and practice the piano, while other parents let their children hang out at the mall and play video games every night. Which parents, down the line, will prove to have been good? To the child, the answer may seem obvious.

But that answer is wrong. ✖

2. Why is it so important for us to recognize that God's goodness has no limits?

✖ God's goodness seen on this fallen Earth is merely a sampling of God's goodness in Heaven.

God promises to ultimately remove all evil so that we will live in a world of utter goodness. Consider this picture of the world where we will live forever: "Now the dwelling of God is with men, and he will live with them. They will be his people, and God himself will be with them and be their God. He will wipe every tear from their eyes. There will be no more death or mourning or crying or pain, for the old order of things has passed away. He who was seated on the throne said, 'I am making everything new!'" (Revelation 21:3–5).

The goodness we see around us now amounts to a whiff of Mama's stew while it simmers on the stove—just a foretaste of the full meal awaiting us.

You and I have never seen men and women as God intended them to be. We've never seen animals as they existed before the Fall. We see only marred remnants of what once was. So if the "wrong side" of Heaven can look so beautiful, what will the "right side" look like? If the smoking ruins appear so stunning, what will Earth look like when God resurrects it and makes it new?

3. Why is the idea of God being limited in goodness an inadequate explanation for why evil and suffering exist in this world?

EXPLORE FURTHER

(For more exploration, review the **bold-text** sentences in *IGIG* chapter 17, and then respond below.)

4. What limits do people sometimes think there are to God's goodness?

5. In this chapter, find and mark the following quoted passages about God's goodness, then summarize the most important truths they teach us: James 1:17; Psalms 25:8; 119:68; Jeremiah 33:11; Nahum 1:7; Psalms 23:6; 65:4; 31:19; 145:9; Acts 14:17; Habakkuk 1:13; Matthew 19:17.

6. Look also at the quoted words in this chapter from Lamentations 3:2–5. How do they illustrate the human reality

and candor of the Bible's writers regarding their view of
God and their suffering?

7. Also find and mark the quoted words from Psalm 119:71,
   75 and 2 Corinthians 12:7–10. What purpose do they
   indicate for the affliction God sometimes sends to his
   people?

8. What most convinces you that God is entirely and consistently good?

9. In regard to God's absolute goodness, what do you now
   feel drawn to praise and worship him for?

10. In this chapter of *IGIG,* as you look over the bold-text
    statements, which one has the most significance right now
    for your life, and why?

● ● ● INVESTIGATE DEEPER

(For more intensive study, read *IGIG* chapter 17.)

11. Explain as fully as you can why it's impossible for God's
    limited goodness to be a solution to the problem of evil
    and suffering.

12. What is the best way to biblically define and understand
    God's goodness? Look up in your Bible Exodus 33:18–19;

34:6–7; and Mark 10:18. How do they inform your answer?

13. Which stories or illustrations in *IGIG* chapter 17 did you find yourself most drawn to, and why?

Is God's Limited Love *a Solution?*
  (See also chapter 18 in *IGIG*, page 177.)

● FOCUS IN

While few critics make a philosophical argument that God lacks love, many, when personally facing evil and suffering, interpret the terrible things happening to them to mean that God doesn't love them after all. Doubt about their salvation may grip them, causing despair.

God's attributes, while varied, work together in complete harmony. If, in our eyes, his holiness contradicts his love or his justice conflicts with his mercy, then that's our problem, not his. The almighty God who created us is the same holy God who condemned us as sinners and the same loving God who went to extraordinary lengths that we might go to Heaven. God's self-consistency demands the simultaneous and full expression of his holiness, his love, and all his other attributes.

● INTERACT

  ✖ God's love *abounds*. It proliferates. It's overflowing, even excessive—something all sufferers need to hear....
  With amazement, John writes, "How great is the love the Father has *lavished* on us, that we should be called children of God! And that is what we are!" (1 John 3:1; see also 4:16). If ever exclamation marks were justified in a translation, surely they are here....

God's constant love for us will never let us down, no matter how things appear. ⚔

1. Why is the idea of God being limited in love an inadequate explanation for why evil and suffering exist in this world?

⚔ Yes, God is love, but it is not his only attribute, nor is it always his defining attribute. More and more we hear that God's love overshadows all his other attributes, as if the rest have only secondary importance....

Unfortunately, this viewpoint guarantees that affirmations of God's holiness or justice, which *also* should never be qualified or compromised, will appear to qualify and compromise God's love....

God cares as much that we share in his holiness as in his love: "God disciplines us for our good, that we may share in his holiness.... Make every effort to live in peace with all men and to be holy; without holiness no one will see the Lord" (Hebrews 12:10, 14).

It's a mistake to think God's love overshadows his holiness, or to think his holiness limits his love. ⚔

2. Why is it so important for us to recognize the full breadth of God's attributes, including both his love and his holiness?

⚔ If God's love outstripped his holiness, then why send Jesus to the cross? If love trumps holiness, then why not dispense with the Crucifixion altogether—especially since Jesus asked for this very thing (see Matthew 26:39)? The truth is, God's holiness and love combined at Calvary constitute the only way possible to save sinners and still satisfy God's perfect nature.

God's love divorced from the full picture of his infinite glory reduces him to a false god, made in our own likeness.

God's love defined in light of the totality of his all-encompassing majesty, depicts him as he truly is and invites our heartfelt praise. ✖

3. In what ways do you see the death of Jesus on the cross as demonstrating both God's love and his holiness?

◦● EXPLORE FURTHER

(For more exploration, review the **bold-text** sentences in *IGIG* chapter 18, and then respond below.)

4. What limits do people sometimes think there are to God's love?

5. In this chapter, find and mark the following quoted passages about God's love, then summarize the most important truths they teach us: Exodus 34:6–7; 2 Chronicles 6:42; Nehemiah 9:17, 32; 1 John 3:1; Romans 5:5; Ephesians 5:1; 1 Thessalonians 1:4; Psalms 32:10; 51:1; Lamentations 3:32; 1 John 4:9–10; Romans 5:8; Isaiah 40:11.

6. Also find and mark the quoted scriptures in this chapter that relate to God's holiness: Exodus 15:11; 1 Samuel 6:20; Psalms 5:4–6; 7:11; 77:13; 99:5, 8–9; Joshua 24:19–20; Mark 1:24; Luke 1:35; Ephesians 4:24; Hebrews 12:10, 14; 1:9; Amos 5:15; John 3:36; Proverbs 8:13. What are the most important factors to keep in mind to help us understand God's holiness?

7. In regard to God's love (as well as his holiness), what do you now feel drawn to praise and worship him for?

8. In this chapter of *IGIG,* as you look over the bold-text statements, which one is most important to you, and why?

⊛ ⊛ ● INVESTIGATE DEEPER

(For more intensive study, read *IGIG* chapter 18.)

9. Explain as fully as you can why it's impossible for God's limited love to be a solution to the problem of evil and suffering.

10. Which stories or illustrations in *IGIG* chapter 18 did you find most memorable, and why?

11. Why is it so important to realize that God's character includes much more than his love?

2-B

The Great Drama

Evil and Suffering in the Great Drama of Christ's Redemptive Work

(Links with section 5 in *If God Is Good,* pages 187–220.)

Evil and Suffering as Seen in Scripture's Redemptive Story

(See also chapter 19 in *IGIG,* page 189.)

FOCUS IN

God's redemptive plan was not an ad-lib response to unanticipated events. From before the very beginning, the Cross of Christ was in the plan of God. The Cross presupposes the Fall of man; it presupposes sin. More importantly, it presupposes God's answer for sin.

God wrote the script of the unfolding drama of redemption long before Satan, demons, Adam and Eve—and you and I—took the stage. And from the beginning, he determined that evil and suffering, brought to their apex in the slaughter of his Son, would bring to pass the greatest demonstration of his grace the world has ever known.

God is not immune to experiencing suffering and having evil inflicted upon him. The plan of redemption is the plan of the incarnation of God into a world of evil in which he would suffer. He would suffer to the ultimate point of death.

INTERACT

The story of redemption began before God created the world.

God speaks of "all whose names have not been written
in the book of life belonging to the Lamb that was slain
from the creation of the world" (Revelation 13:8). Before
creation itself, God had written myriad names in the book
of life. That book belongs to "the Lamb that was slain." Before God took his first step in forming this universe, already
he had determined to sacrifice his Son for our sins, like a
lamb on the sacrificial altar.

From the perspective of a timeless God, Christ's sufferings and death did not confine themselves to a few years
or hours. Before the world fell—even before he created
it—God knew *exactly* what he would do to redeem the
world. He knew the horrors of evil before Adam and Eve
knew them. When you consider that the distant future is as
real to God as the present is to us, then this passage takes
on paradigm-shifting meaning. ❧

1. What do you want *your* part to be in this story of redemption that God began so long ago, and is still unfolding?
   What words would you use to describe it?

❧ Like Job, we live in a cosmic drama, in full view of
Heaven's audience.

In the first chapter of Job, the drama's Director tells us
what the characters don't know—what's *really* going on.
Job knew nothing about God commending Job to Satan and
calling him blameless. God let Job face terrible trials with
no explanation.

We share this in common with Job—*God doesn't specif-
ically explain why he permits evil and suffering to fall upon us.*
He wants us to trust him. ❧

2. It's been said that every trial is a "trust test." As you consider "the patience of Job" (James 5:11, KJV), how is God

calling you to trust him, even in circumstances you don't fully understand?

�֍ While in the larger story this is not the best possible world, it may be the best possible means of achieving the best possible world....

If you tell God he should not have allowed evil and suffering, then you are saying he should not have allowed us to experience compassion, mercy, and sacrificial love. In order for those characteristics to develop and become part of us, God had to permit evil and suffering. Can we fault God for ordaining the kind of world in which we could experience such great good?...

If God merely wanted to develop men and women who would behave correctly, he could have bypassed freedom, evil, and suffering. But if he intended that his image-bearers see their genuine need for him and be brought to loving obedience, then how would we propose that he improve the processes he uses in our lives? ֍

3. Which of these do you think God appreciates most in you and why: your "correct behavior" or your gratitude for his mercy and compassion?

EXPLORE FURTHER

(For more exploration, review the **bold-text** sentences in *IGIG* chapter 19, and then respond to the following questions.)

4. In what ways is the Bible the ultimate *story*, and the source and pattern for all other true stories?

5. In this chapter, find and mark each of the following quoted passages, then summarize what they add to the great dramatic story of God's redemption of mankind: Revelation 13:8; 2 Timothy 1:9; Genesis 6:5; 8:21; 11:4; 22:18; 2 Peter 3:9; Revelation 7:9; 5:9–10; 2 Thessalonians 2:3, 6–7; Exodus 3:7–10.

6. Look also at these quoted scriptures: Psalms 56:8; 103:13; Ephesians 4:30; Deuteronomy 1:37; Judges 2:18; 1 Kings 3:10; Zephaniah 3:17; Genesis 6:6; Exodus 32:10; Isaiah 54:8; 62:5; Jeremiah 48:31; Isaiah 63:9. Together, what do they tell us about God's emotions as well as our own?

7. In this chapter of *IGIG,* as you look over the bold-text statements, which one has the most significance right now for your life, and why?

◦ ◦ ● INVESTIGATE DEEPER
(For more intensive study, read *IGIG* chapter 19.)

8. How would you summarize the highlights and critical turning points of God's redemptive story?

If You Were the Author, How Would You Have Written the Story?
(See also chapter 20 in *IGIG,* page 196.)

◦ FOCUS IN
As a member of the real-life story's cast, you might wish for a world untouched by evil and suffering. That's understandable, because life is hard as the story unfolds; and it *will* be hard until it culminates or you leave the stage, having played your part.

But if you were sitting in the audience, which story would you prefer to watch? And if you were writing the story, which version would you prefer to write? And even as a cast member, having endured such difficulty, ten thousand years from now at the ongoing cast party in honor of the Writer and Director, when grand tales make the rounds at dinner tables on the New Earth—which story do you think you would vote for?

"All's well that ends well" is a cliché, but there's truth in it. There's no substitute for a happy ending. And the happiest endings are the ones that overcome the greatest odds to get there.

⬡ INTERACT

✖ Parents who try to make their children happy in the short term unwisely allow their children to set the agenda. Children question even the best parent's goodness and love. "Why can't I have ice cream? I don't want to go to bed. I want to watch this movie. Why can't I?" Notice the key-word in the questioning of parental authority, wisdom, and goodness: *Why?*

Why also dominates our thinking in the problem of evil and suffering. If God is good, *why* does he let us suffer? *Why* doesn't he stop the things that make us unhappy? Or as the child puts it, *why* doesn't he let us eat what we want, *why* doesn't he let us go where we want? *Why* does he discipline us?...

What if forever attaining the highest good in the universe means *not* getting what we think we want now? What if the highest good means learning to trust God and becoming more Christlike? What if the Author chose the right setting and plot twists after all, and in the end we'll be eternally grateful for our God-given part in the story? ✖

1. What is the "highest good" you believe God wants you to experience in the full eternal story of your life?

✶ How long will we need to be in Heaven before our new home will make up for all the suffering we've faced in this life? Two months? Two weeks? Two days? Two hours? Two minutes?

The bleakest pessimist might answer, "More like a hundred years." But even if you say ten *thousand* years, that will be but the beginning of an eternal life of joy and pleasures at God's right hand (see Psalm 16:11). When we realize God has promised us a redeemed universe and time without end, we'll finally "get it." We'll have opportunity to develop and fulfill dreams bigger than anything we ever had on this fallen Earth. Heaven will be anything but boring! ✦

2. Have you thought that Heaven might be boring? If so, what caused you to think that way?

⦿ ● EXPLORE FURTHER

(For more exploration, review the **bold-text** sentences in *IGIG* chapter 20, and then answer the following questions.)

3. What would you say are the strongest elements of any good story?

4. How would you answer the question in this chapter's title: if you were the author, how would you have written the story?

5. What is most satisfying to you about the story the Bible tells?

6. In this chapter of *IGIG,* as you look over the bold-text statements, which one has the most significance right now for your life, and why?

◦ ◦ ● INVESTIGATE DEEPER
(For more intensive study, read *IGIG* chapter 20.)

7. For you personally, how helpful is it to focus on the Bible's teaching as an epic story?

8. Which stories or illustrations in *IGIG* chapter 20 did you find yourself most drawn to, and why?

Jesus: The Only Answer Bigger Than the Questions
(See also chapter 21 in *IGIG,* page 206.)

◦ FOCUS IN
The Cross is God's answer to the question, "Why don't you do something about evil?"

But what if God *did* do something about it? What if what he did was so great and unprecedented that it shook the angelic realm's foundation, and ripped in half, from the top down, not only the temple curtain but the fabric of the universe itself?

A powerful moment in the movie *The Passion of the Christ* occurs when Jesus, overwhelmed with pain and exhaustion, lies on the ground as guards kick, mock, and spit on him. A horrified woman, her hand outstretched, pleads, "Someone, stop this!"

The great irony is that "Someone," God's Son, was doing something unspeakably great that required it *not* be stopped.

Had someone delivered Jesus from his suffering that day, he could not now deliver us from ours.

◉ INTERACT

✖ God allowed Jesus' temporary suffering so he could prevent our eternal suffering....

Christ's atonement guarantees the final end of evil and suffering....

The drama of evil and suffering in Christ's sacrifice addresses the very heart of the problem of evil and suffering. One day it will prove to have been the final answer. ✖

1. In what ways is Christ's suffering the "final answer" to our own human suffering, and why will this be fully understood by us only in the future?

✖ The Cross exposes us for what we are. The punishment our evil warrants answers the question "How evil are we?" The Cross is a mirror showing us the heart-stopping magnitude of our depravity and offers a terrible glimpse of Hell's misery....

God's love comes to us soaked in divine blood. One look at Jesus—at his incarnation and the redemption he provided us—should silence the argument that God has withdrawn to some far corner of the universe where he keeps his hands clean and maintains his distance from human suffering.

God does not merely empathize with our sufferings. He actually suffers. Jesus is God. What Jesus suffered, God suffered. ✖

2. What is it about the Cross that exemplifies so completely the worst of human suffering?

✖ If I had to believe that what we now see represents God's best for this world, I would not be a Christian. If not for the redemptive work of Christ, I would not believe in God's goodness. The fault would lie with me, for God would remain good even if he hadn't gone to the cross for us. But no matter how persuasive the argument that we sinners deserve judgment, I couldn't overcome the obstacles of suffering children, or slaughters like the Holocaust and Killing Fields.

That Jesus Christ, the eternal Son of God, would choose to endure the holocaust of the Cross to pay for sin, that he would take on the sufferings of *all* people in Golgotha's Killing Field, changed the way I look at suffering and evil, and how they reflect upon God's character.

For me, Jesus changes everything. ✠

3. In what ways have you found your own views of suffering changed by your understanding of Jesus and what he did on the cross?

✠ Whenever you feel tempted to ask God, "Why did you do this *to* me?" look at the Cross and ask, "Why did you do that *for* me?"...

History's worst event happened to history's best person....

In his haunting cry, "Why have you forsaken me?" Christ identifies with our despair....

When Jesus cried, "My God, my God, why have you forsaken me?" he bridged the gap between God and us not only theologically, in the Atonement, but emotionally, between our suffering and God's, between our agonizing cries and God's.

How could he endure such suffering for us? And why, since he has done so, would I ever accuse or reject him? ✠

4. How would you respond to the questions Randy asks in
   the previous paragraph?

�֎ When we feel upset with God and tempted to blame
him, we should look at the outstretched arms of Jesus and
focus on his wounds, not ours....

   If God can use the horror of Christ's crucifixion for
good, then surely he can use our suffering for good.

   Christ foresaw the good even as he faced the bad, and
that helped him to endure the bad: "[Jesus] who for the joy
set before him endured the cross, scorning its shame, and sat
down at the right hand of the throne of God" (Hebrews 12:2).

   If God brought eternal joy through the suffering of
Jesus, can he bring eternal joy through my present suffering, and yours? If Jesus endured his suffering through an-
ticipating the reward of unending joy, can he empower you
and me to do the same? ֎

5. Again, how would you respond to those questions in
   the paragraph above? And what does this mean for you
   personally?

●● EXPLORE FURTHER

(For more exploration, review the **bold-text** sentences in *IGIG* chapter 21,
and then respond below.)

6. In this chapter, look for the following quoted passages, and
   relate what they communicate to you about Christ's humanity and vulnerability: Isaiah 53:2; Matthew 8:20;
   26:38; 26:53; John 7:12; Hebrews 4:15; Luke 22:44; John
   12:27–28.

7. Look also at these two quoted scriptures: Job 9:32–34 and
   1 Timothy 2:5. Explain what it means in the Timothy passage that Christ is our "mediator."

8. Also, find and mark these quoted passages, and tell what
   they communicate most to your own heart about the love
   of God as proven in Christ's death on the cross: Isaiah
   52:13–53:12; John 10:15, 17–18; 2 Corinthians 5:21;
   Philippians 2:7–8; 1 Peter 3:18; 1 John 4:10; Luke 23:46;
   Hebrews 12:2.

9. Finally, look also for these quoted passages, mark them,
   and accept them as the Lord's words of invitation to you
   and to everyone you will ever know: John 14:6; Acts 4:12;
   Matthew 16:16; Psalms 66:5; 34:8; John 1:45–46.

10. In this chapter of *IGIG,* as you look over the bold-text
    statements, which one means the most to you, and why?

◉ ◉ ● **INVESTIGATE DEEPER**
(For more intensive study, read *IGIG* chapter 21.)

11. Do you think it's true that Jesus is an "answer bigger" than
    our questions, as this chapter's title says? If so, in what ways
    is he "bigger"?

12. Why is the Cross so central to the Bible's overall story?

13. Which stories or illustrations in *IGIG* chapter 21 did you find yourself most drawn to, and why?

PART 3

God at Work

(Links with sections 6–8 in If God Is Good, *pages 221–358)*

3-A

Who's in Control?

DIVINE SOVEREIGNTY AND MEANINGFUL HUMAN CHOICE: ACCOUNTING FOR EVIL AND SUFFERING

(Links with section 6 in *If God Is Good,* pages 221–90.)

God's Sovereignty and Its Reach
(See also chapter 22 in *IGIG,* page 225.)

❋ FOCUS IN

God didn't devise his redemptive plan on the fly. Evil didn't take him by surprise. God isn't the author of evil, but the author of a story that *includes* evil. He intended from the beginning to permit evil, then to turn evil on its head, to take what evil angels and evil people intended for evil and use it for good. In the face of the lowest evil, God intended to show his highest good.

It's possible to plan for something you know is coming without forcing that thing to happen. God didn't force Adam and Eve to do evil, but he did create them with freedom and permitted Satan's presence in the garden, knowing they would choose evil and knowing that what he would do in his redemptive plan would serve a greater good.

❋ INTERACT

   ✖ God's sovereignty gives him ownership and authority over the universe.

      God's sovereignty is the biblical teaching that all things remain under God's rule and nothing happens without either his direction or permission. God works in all things for the good of his children (see Romans 8:28). These "all things" include evil and suffering. God doesn't commit moral evil, but he can use any evil for good purposes....

[God]..."works out everything in conformity with the purpose of his will," wrote Paul (Ephesians 1:11).

"Everything" is comprehensive, allowing for no exceptions. God works even in those things done against his moral will, to bring them into conformity with his purpose and according to his plan. God can and will redeem the worst thing that ever happens to his child. ⚔

1. How is it possible for God to actually be "working" in this world of evil and suffering? What does it mean that he "redeems" these bad things?

⚔ The proud human heart doesn't want to submit to almighty God. We want to make our own plans, do our own thing, and have it our way. We don't want anyone, including God, to impose his way on us....

We delude ourselves when we think we have ultimate control over our lives. We imagine that God should let us have our way. And when he doesn't, we resent him. ⚔

2. How have you experienced the kind of heart resistance that "doesn't want to submit to almighty God"?

⚔ God is both loving and sovereign.... Knowing this should give us great confidence that even when we don't see any redemptive meaning in our suffering, *God* can see it—and one day we will too. Therefore, we need not run from suffering or lose hope if God doesn't remove it. We can trust that God has a purpose for whatever he permits.

Perhaps the greatest test of whether we believe Romans 8:28 ["For those who love God all things work together for good, for those who are called according to his purpose" (ESV)] is to identify the very worst things that have happened to us, and then ask if we believe that, in the end, God will somehow use them for our good. ⚔

3. Make lists of the best and the worst things that have happened in your life. Compare the two. Chances are you will see a surprising overlap between them. Based on your past experience, how strongly do you believe that God will in the end somehow use tough times for your good?

● ● EXPLORE FURTHER

(For more exploration, review the **bold-text** sentences in *IGIG* chapter 22, and then answer the following questions.)

4. How would you explain the term *sovereignty of God*? What does it mean to you?

5. This chapter quotes a number of Scripture passages that tell us about God's sovereignty. Find and mark those on the following list, and summarize *what you consider to be their most important teachings:* Psalm 22:28; Hebrews 1:3; Ephesians 1:11; Matthew 16:21; Mark 13:7; 13:10; Luke 17:25; 24:26; Revelation 13:8; Ephesians 1:4–5; Acts 2:23; 1 Timothy 6:15; 1 Chronicles 29:12; Job 23:13; Daniel 4:17; Proverbs 16:33; Matthew 10:29–30; Genesis 45:5–8; 50:20; 15:13; Isaiah 46:10; Daniel 4:35; 1 Samuel 1:5; Psalm 139:13; 1 Samuel 2:7–8; John 19:10–11; Acts 17:25–26; Exodus 4:11; James 4:13–16; Romans 8:28.

6. In this chapter of *IGIG,* as you look over the bold-text statements, which one has the most significance for your life, and why?

●●● INVESTIGATE DEEPER
(For more intensive study, read *IGIG* chapter 22.)

7. From what Scripture teaches us, how far does God's sovereignty actually "reach," as the chapter title puts it?

8. Which stories or illustrations in *IGIG* chapter 22 did you find most inspiring, and why?

9. What unanswered questions do you have about God's sovereignty?

"Free Will" and Meaningful Choice
(See also chapter 23 in *IGIG,* page 238.)

● FOCUS IN
God is intelligent, creative, communicative, and free to choose. To be made in his likeness, then, likely includes having these attributes, though on a finite level. We visibly reflect the invisible God. We think because he thinks, we speak because he speaks, we create because he creates, and we choose because he chooses. These things all come from God and comprise part of what it means to be human.

God sovereignly created angels and human beings with an ability to make real choices. Their wills were uncoerced; they were at liberty to choose obedience or sin, life or death. Yet God was never surprised, nor did the sinful choices of his creatures thwart his predetermined plans. People make their choices freely, within the confines of their nature. And God, according to his divine nature, brings to pass his gracious and holy will.

❋ INTERACT

✛ The term "free will" misleads when applied to slaves of sin.

Our free will is limited first because we are finite. Even when morally perfect, Adam and Eve were not free to choose to do whatever came into their mind…. There are a lot of things they weren't smart enough or strong enough to do. God alone is infinite, and therefore *God alone has completely free will* that permits him to do whatever he wants (and which will always be in keeping with his flawless character).

What may be less obvious to us is that *our* free will is far more limited still due to our sin natures. *We are not just finite, we are fallen….*

Sinners do not have the freedom to choose in exactly the same way as Adam and Eve did. Freedom still exists, but our fallenness greatly limits our capacity to obey God. Scripture tells us, and experience confirms, that sin holds us in bondage….

Paul wrestles with the reality that even the regenerate person feels inclined toward evil: "When I want to do good, evil is right there with me…. What a wretched man I am! Who will rescue me from this body of death? Thanks be to God—through Jesus Christ our Lord! So then, I myself in my mind am a slave to God's law, but in the sinful nature a slave to the law of sin" (Romans 7:21, 24–25). ✛

1. How does the fact that we are finite and fallen creatures limit our freedom as human beings?

� While Scripture reveals truths such as sovereignty, election, and predestination, it doesn't reveal the reality of human choice as much as it simply *assumes* it, but it does so repeatedly. It's as if something so self-evident as our ability to make choices doesn't require special revelation or commentary. *Of course* we can choose. We do so constantly....

Surely we all must believe in *some* degree of meaningful human choice, both for believers and unbelievers....

If meaningful choice does not exist, then life isn't real. ✖

2. Give an example of what Randy is talking about. What are some of the "meaningful choices," small or large, that you've made in the past few hours?

✖ Our real but limited freedom is instinctively misdirected and dangerous....

[God] speaks of our fallen condition: "The heart is deceitful above all things, and desperately sick; who can understand it?" (Jeremiah 17:9, ESV).

We may freely follow our desires, but this is not entirely good news. Why not? Because *we lack freedom to dictate our desires.* We are not innocent beings inclined to choose whatever's best. We are not even morally neutral beings, objectively weighing and measuring our options. We are congenitally selfish....

How free are we? Free enough to be human, free enough to be morally responsible and accountable, free enough to make consequential choices that matter. Free enough to make choices, some better and some worse—yet not free enough to transform our own hearts or make ourselves righteous before God. ✖

3. If we're not free to make ourselves righteous, what does God require of us that we might have new life in him? (Look up in your Bible John 6:28–29 and Ephesians 2:8–9.)

⬡● EXPLORE FURTHER

(For more exploration, review the **bold-text** sentences in *IGIG* chapter 23, and then respond to the following questions.)

4. This chapter quotes Scripture passages that tell us about our capacity for meaningful choice (or "free will"). Find and mark the passages in the following list, then summarize *what you consider to be their most important teachings:* Genesis 2:16–17; 3:13; John 8:34; Romans 6:20, 22; 7:21, 24–25; John 6:44; Deuteronomy 30:11–14, 19–20; Ezekiel 33:11; Proverbs 4:13–15; Joshua 24:15; Deuteronomy 23:16; James 4:4; 1 Peter 4:3; Genesis 22:12; Exodus 16:4; Isaiah 1:16–20; Jeremiah 13:23; 17:9; Mark 7:21–23; Romans 8:9.

5. What seems to be the best way to explain and understand human free will from a biblical perspective?

6. In this chapter of *IGIG,* as you look over the bold-text statements, which one has the most significance for your own life, and why?

⬡●● INVESTIGATE DEEPER

(For more intensive study, read *IGIG* chapter 23.)

7. How would you summarize the main arguments in the free-will debate, as discussed in this chapter?

8. What is the best way to understand biblically the term *free will*?

9. Which stories or illustrations in *IGIG* chapter 23 seemed most important to you, and why?

This World's Structure Is Necessary for Meaningful Choice
(See also chapter 24 in *IGIG*, page 251.)

❂ FOCUS IN
Meaningful choice requires a cause-and-effect system in which choices generate consequences.

I've heard people argue that a good and all-powerful God should miraculously intervene every time someone intends to do harm.

If God disarmed every shooter and prevented every drunk driver from crashing, this wouldn't be a real world in which people make consequential choices. It wouldn't be a world of character development and faith building. It wouldn't be a world where families put their arms around one another to face life's difficulties. It would be a world where people went blithely along with their lives, content to do evil and put up with it, feeling no need to turn to God, no incentive to consider the gospel and prepare for eternity. In such a world, people would die without a sense of need, only to find themselves in Hell.

❂ INTERACT
✖ God could not make human beings while eliminating the process by which humans mature; he could create us innocent, but we must *become* righteous.

We come into the world as infants, gradually growing physically and mentally. We learn by experience.... Even Adam and Eve, though created innocent, weren't created wise. They needed to grow in understanding.

Scripture teaches a continuity of our identity from this life to the next. For us to become the best people we can be for eternity, something needs to happen in us while we live here. As we move through a world of choice and consequences, we need to come to see God for who he is and his goodness for what it is. ⚔

1. How conscious are you that God is using your life experiences, both good and bad, to help prepare you for your eternal dwelling place?

⚔ To argue that God should not permit evil or suffering is to argue against not only human choice, but love. In other words, a world without the choice to hate would be a world without the choice to love....

Forced love is no love at all. Love requires the freedom not to love. ⚔

2. Why is freedom required before true love can exist? How do you see that truth in your own love relationships?

⬤⬤ EXPLORE FURTHER

(For more exploration, review the **bold-text** sentences in *IGIG* chapter 24, and then respond below.)

3. Explain how cause and effect works in this world, especially in relation to moral choices.

4. In this chapter, find and mark the words from Romans 9:19–21. How do they indicate that God's "free will" supersedes that of man's?

5. In this chapter of *IGIG,* as you look over the bold-text statements, which has the most significance for your own life, and why?

●●● INVESTIGATE DEEPER
(For more intensive study, read *IGIG* chapter 24.)

6. Why is this world's structure necessary for meaningful human choice?

7. Randy states, "Doing good is always smart while doing evil is always stupid" (page 251). Philosophically and biblically, why is this statement true?

8. Which stories or illustrations in *IGIG* chapter 24 did you find yourself most drawn to, and why?

9. Find the following passages in your Bible, and record how they indicate the necessity of a cause-and-effect system for meaningful human choice: 1 Corinthians 3:12–15; Galatians 6:7; 1 Timothy 5:24; 2 Peter 3:11–14; 2 John 8.

Meaningful Human Choice and Divine Sovereignty Working Together
(See also chapter 25 in *IGIG,* page 258.)

● FOCUS IN
Our problem is both our unwillingness to understand *and* our incapacity to turn our wills toward God. Once we grasp the depths of this problem,

we'll fully appreciate the wonders of his grace. Without that insight, we might imagine ourselves in Heaven congratulating one another that we had the savvy and strength of will to turn to Christ. But God leaves no room for such boasting (see Ephesians 2:8–9).

God's amazing grace doesn't end at our conversion. Even the regenerated human will depends upon the divine will to live as it should. Philippians 2:12–13 speaks both to those who understate and those who overstate the role of the human will: "Continue to work out your salvation with fear and trembling, for it is God who works in you to will and to act according to his good purpose." We must will and work, *and* God must will and work.

❋ INTERACT

❖ Clearly,...the world as it exists *now* does not qualify as the best possible world. For it is neither as God created it nor as it one day will be. It was once better and it will eventually be better. It is at most the best possible world *under the circumstances,* those circumstances being that it is fallen. But even then it would seem that a single evil removed from this world or a single good added to it could make it a better world....

God has hung a sign on this Earth that says, "Condemned: Plans in place for radical restoration, to begin soon. Come back and see. You'll love it." ❖

1. How could God use you to help make this a better world?

❖ God's invitation to come to him assumes the possibility of a real and meaningful choice to accept it.

"Come to me," Jesus says, "all you who are weary and burdened, and I will give you rest" (Matthew 11:28)....

Jesus goes on to say, "No one can come to me unless the Father who sent him draws him" (John 6:44)....

Apparently we freely choose Christ because he empowers us to do so. That may not make sense to us, but when we compare all scriptures, discarding none, that seems to be the truth.

People genuinely respond to God, yet God first opens their hearts....

Still...God extends a *genuine,* not a *pretend* invitation to choice-making people to come to him. They can do so as he sovereignly empowers them....

Sinners should choose to repent, yet only God grants saving repentance. God calls upon us not only to surrender and lay down our arms, but to switch sides. We need his empowerment to do this. ✣

2. Explain in your own words these seemingly contradictory truths: we can choose to become a Christian, yet it's God himself who enables that choice. Why is it important to understand and accept both these truths?

✣ Scripture does not teach that God wills everything, in the sense that he forces everything or is pleased with everything that happens in this fallen world....

Scripture teaches that humans make real choices and that we must resist evil, yet God remains sovereign in a nonfatalistic way, offering us choices and encouraging us to pray for him to bring changes, and to do what we can to change our lives and the world itself. This may confuse us, but the Bible plainly teaches both truths. ✣

3. What are the most important things God wants you to do *today,* at this moment in your life, in consciously choosing to follow him and to resist evil?

⊛ ⊛ EXPLORE FURTHER

(For more exploration, review the **bold-text** sentences in *IGIG* chapter 25, and then respond to the following questions.)

4. How can it simultaneously be true that human beings have meaningful choice and God is in control?

5. Mark the following quoted passages in this chapter, and state in your own words how together they indicate the way our meaningful choice (free will) is an active reality, even under divine sovereignty: Matthew 11:28; Revelation 22:17; Acts 16:14; Colossians 2:13; John 12:32; 5:21; 2 Timothy 2:25–26; Romans 8:7; Philippians 2:12–13; Ephesians 1:11; Matthew 6:10; 1 Timothy 2:4; Matthew 23:37; Isaiah 63:10; Acts 7:51; Romans 9:16; Psalms 33:10–11; 115:3; Proverbs 16:4.

6. In this chapter of *IGIG,* as you look over the bold-text statements, which one seems most important to you right now, and why?

⊛ ⊛ ⊛ INVESTIGATE DEEPER

(For more intensive study, read *IGIG* chapter 25.)

7. What further questions do you have about the combination of meaningful human choice and divine sovereignty?

8. Review Randy's description (page 264) of *determinism, libertarianism,* and *compatibilism.* How would you explain each of these?

9. Describe the freedom that will be ours in Heaven.

10. Which stories or illustrations in *IGIG* chapter 25 did you find most valuable, and why?

Further Thoughts on God's Sovereignty and Human Will
(See also chapter 26 in *IGIG*, page 271.)

❋ FOCUS IN

We can believe in God's sovereignty and still lock the door. "If a man is lazy," says Ecclesiastes, "the rafters sag; if his hands are idle, the house leaks" (10:18).

These verses don't attribute sagging rafters and leaking houses to God's sovereignty. They lay responsibility on people to take action. Students who don't study and set the alarm to get up for class aren't trusting God; they're just being irresponsible.

No contradiction exists between praying, "Lord, please protect us and the children on this drive," and then putting on seat belts. Prayers for healing do not conflict with the common grace of medical treatment. Why should we choose between the two? Believers understand that receiving medical treatment before, after, and while we pray for the sick helps them in two vital ways.

❋ INTERACT

↔ God's purpose and glory are the life-breath of the universe. Everything—including the real choices that Satan, angels, and every person makes—is subordinate to God's redemptive plan, which he carries out with deliberate purpose.

If anything in the universe can happen outside of God's control, then ultimately we can't trust his promises....

The Bible overflows with promises. But if things happen outside the sovereign control of God, how can he guarantee those promises will be kept? ✖

1. What promises from God mean the most to you? Why must God be in ultimate control for those promises to be fulfilled?

✖ God holds men accountable for the sin they choose to do. But it is not inconsistent or unjust of him to utilize their low-purposed, finite evil for his high-purposed, infinite good.

This reality should prompt us to worship him for his greatness and his ability to use even what displeases him to accomplish what will ultimately please both him and us. Our fates do not rest with people who file lawsuits against us, or with unjust politicians, lawyers, teachers, coaches, military officers, or employers. They can do their worst against us—and God is fully capable of turning it around and using it for our best (no matter how much it hurts in the meantime)....

God's sovereign grace and ability to use evil doesn't justify or minimize evildoing, it simply shows that he is infinitely superior to any evildoer and that his plan to do good to his people will not be derailed by *any* creature. ✖

2. What evil circumstances or events are the hardest for you to accept as being something God can use to accomplish good?

⊛⊛ EXPLORE FURTHER

(For more exploration, review the **bold-text** sentences in *IGIG* chapter 26, and then answer the following questions.)

3. What is the relationship between God's sovereignty and our ability to trust his promises?

4. Find and mark the following quoted passages from this chapter: Psalm 90:11; Jeremiah 21:5; Romans 3:7–8. How do they demonstrate God's anger toward and opposition of sin?

5. Look also at these quoted scriptures in this chapter: 2 Chronicles 10:15; Acts 13:48; 14:1; 1 Corinthians 9:19, 22. How do they demonstrate both God's sovereignty *and* meaningful human choice?

6. In this chapter of *IGIG,* as you look over the bold-text statements, which one is most significant to you right now, and why?

◉ ◉ ● INVESTIGATE DEEPER
(For more intensive study, read *IGIG* chapter 26.)

7. Are you fully convinced that God's sovereignty is biblically consistent with human responsibility? Why or why not?

8. Which stories or illustrations in *IGIG* chapter 26 did you find yourself most drawn to, and why?

The God Who Brings Good Out of Bad
(See also chapter 27 in *IGIG,* page 282.)

✸ FOCUS IN

God's glory is the highest good of the universe. His permitting evil and suffering—and paying the price to end them—will ultimately reveal his character and cause his people to worship him forever.

If we recognize God's sovereignty even over Satan's work, it changes our perspective.

You might not know whether demons, or human genetics under the Fall, or a doctor's poor decision, or God's direct hand have brought about your disease, but you know as much as you need to—that God is sovereign, and whether he heals you now or waits until the resurrection, he desires to achieve his own good purpose in you.

If the world is as random as some theologians suggest, it would seem that people, demons, and luck determine our destinies. We can drive ourselves crazy with such thoughts—or embrace God's higher purpose in painful and even tragic events.

✸ INTERACT

✠ Satan and God intend the same suffering for entirely different purposes, but God's purpose triumphs....

Satan intends your suffering for evil; God intends it for good.

Whose purpose in your suffering will prevail? Whose purpose are you furthering?

Satan attempts to destroy your faith, while God invites you to draw near to him and draw upon his sovereign grace to sustain you. ✠

1. When you're personally experiencing hardship, what kind of responses will further Satan's purposes? And what kind will further God's purposes?

✠ Countless millions of choices and actions are contemplated every instant across this globe. Our all-knowing and all-powerful God chooses exactly which ones he will permit and not permit. Scripture suggests he does not per-mit evils arbitrarily, but with specific purposes in mind. Everything he permits matches up with his wisdom and ultimately serves both his holiness and his love.

God "permitting" something, then, describes what is far stronger than it may sound. After all, whatever God permits actually happens; what he doesn't permit doesn't happen....

Many find this truth disturbing, but properly under-stood it should be comforting. What should be disturbing is the notion that God stands passively by while Satan, evildo-ers, diseases, and random accidents ruin the lives of his beloved children. ⚔

2. When you consider the fact that in any single moment, God really does oversee all the countless choices and ac-tions taking place, is this disturbing to you, or comforting? And why?

⚔ The greater the obstacles, the greater the glory to God.

We see something remarkable about a person who can bring some good out of bad. But most remarkable is to bring something incredibly good out of something desper-ately bad. To redeem what appears irredeemable magni-fies the greatness of the Redeemer. If the universe exists to demonstrate God's infinite greatness, then shouldn't we expect God to scale the highest redemptive mountain? The problems of death, evil, and suffering must be vast in order for God to show his superior greatness.

Every time we ask God to remove some obstacle in our lives, we should realize we may be asking him to forgo one more opportunity to declare his greatness. Certainly he sometimes graciously answers our prayers to relieve our suffering. This too testifies to his greatness, and we should praise him for answering. But when he answers no, we should recognize that he desires to demonstrate his greater glory. May we then bend our knees and trust his sovereign grace. ❧

3. What are the worst situations of evil and suffering you are aware of? And how strong is your conviction that these will be the situations that bring the most glory to God?

◦● EXPLORE FURTHER

(For more exploration, review the **bold-text** sentences in *IGIG* chapter 27, and then respond to the questions below.)

4. What kinds of things do you think are really *good* for you, from God's perspective?

5. In this chapter, find and mark where Romans 8:28 is quoted. What does the "all things" in this passage include when it comes to evil and suffering?

6. In this chapter of *IGIG,* as you look over the bold-text statements, which one has the most significance for your life, and why?

◦●● INVESTIGATE DEEPER

(For more intensive study, read *IGIG* chapter 27.)

7. How has God proven that he can bring good out of bad?

8. In Genesis 50, God allowed Joseph to see how the "all things" in his life had been turned to good. But we may

not see that same promise of Romans 8:28 fulfilled in our lifetime. What reasons might God have for not always revealing how the bad things that happen in our lives will be turned to good?

9. Which stories or illustrations in *IGIG* chapter 27 did you find most helpful, and why?

3-B

Eternal Perspectives

THE TWO ETERNAL SOLUTIONS TO THE PROBLEM OF EVIL: HEAVEN AND HELL

(Links with section 7 in *If God Is Good,* pages 291–323.)

Heaven: Eternal Grace to Unworthy but Grateful Children
(See also chapter 28 in *IGIG,* page 293.)

⬡ FOCUS IN

Here, we have bodies and we work, rest, play, and relate to one another—we call this *life.* Yet many have mistakenly redefined *eternal life* to mean an off-Earth disembodied existence stripped of human life's defining properties. Eternal life will mean enjoying forever, as resurrected (which means embodied) beings, what life on Earth at its finest offered us. We could more accurately call our present existence the *beforelife* rather than calling Heaven the *afterlife.* Life doesn't merely continue in Heaven; it emerges at last to its intended fullness.

How will we feel when the great shadow departs forever?

How will we feel when everything happy comes true, and everything sad comes untrue?

Perhaps we'll feel like it couldn't get any better than that.

But each new day will prove us wrong.

⬡ INTERACT

✣ Jesus said that when his followers hunger, weep, and

are hated and insulted, we should rejoice. Why? "Because great is your reward in heaven" (Luke 6:23).

In contrast, he added, "But woe to you who are rich, for you have already received your comfort. Woe to you who are well fed now, for you will go hungry. Woe to you who laugh now, for you will mourn and weep" (verses 24–25).

His listeners would have immediately understood that he was addressing a fundamental problem of human existence, the same one that *If God Is Good* is all about. Christ's point? God has an eternal two-part solution to the problem of the righteous presently suffering and the wicked presently prospering: Heaven and Hell. ❧

1. When you think of the terms *Heaven* and *Hell,* what images come to mind?

❧ If Heaven did not exist, we could never solve the problem of evil and suffering, for we would never receive any lasting compensation for it....

We want every chapter of our lives to feel good. It doesn't work that way. The current chapter may be terribly hard, but the story hasn't ended. God promises a final chapter in which he ties together all the story's loose ends and launches us into an eternal sequel of incredibly grand proportions.

Make no mistake—the promise of God is that *all* his children,...*[all]* who know Jesus, will live happily ever after. ❧

2. Do you tend to live each day with the sense your life is moving toward a happily-ever-after eternity? What difference should that kind of attitude make in a person's life?

❧ When the New Testament discusses suffering, it repeatedly puts Heaven before the eyes of believers. Sadly, many churches fail to follow this example. When we say nothing, or put our hope in a health and wealth gospel, or hope only in medical advances, we rob God's people of an eternal perspective....

As Romans 8:18 emphasizes, our present sufferings are not worth comparing to the future glory that God and we and others will see in us.

Paul offers a one-word answer to the question, "Why suffering?" He replies, "Glory." Glory is a state of high honor, involving a brilliant, radiant beauty. Our glory is secondary, not primary. We are not its source, God is. He is the sun who shines upon us, bestowing an eternal glory rooted in himself, purchased for us by his suffering on the cross. God will be glorified by imparting his honor to us and sharing it with us.

God's promise of glory doesn't minimize our suffering, of course; Paul affirms we will experience great sufferings (see Romans 8). Only an immeasurably greater glory can eclipse our present suffering—and that is exactly what will happen. Romans 8:18 says God will not *create* that glory, but will *reveal* it. It's already there—just not yet manifested....

We can rejoice now because Christ promised that in Heaven he will replace our weeping with laughter; our poverty with wealth; our hunger with satisfaction; and hatred, insults, and rejection with eternal reward. ❧

3. Why is it so important that we always include eternity in our perspective when we're considering present-day evil and suffering?

� Failing to grasp God's promises concerning the world to come sets us up for both discouragement and sin. We tell ourselves, *If I don't experience an intimate friendship now, I never will.* Or, *If I can't afford to travel to that beautiful place now, I never will.* We feel desperate to get what we *think* we want. So we're tempted toward fornication, indebtedness, or theft.

But if we understand both the negative truth that God will judge all sin and the positive truth that we'll actually live in a new universe full of new opportunities, then we can forgo certain pleasures and experiences *now,* knowing we can enjoy far greater ones *later.*

Jesus sees nothing wrong in looking forward to rewards—he assures those caring for the poor "you will be repaid at the resurrection" (see Luke 14:12–14). But we should look for that reward from God in the next life rather than from people in this one. Jesus said we will enjoy forever in Heaven the treasures we lay up now (see Matthew 6:19–20).

What excites and interests you most? A new car? A chance to get rich? An attractive person? A vacation? Or being with God and his people on the New Earth? ✕

4. How would you honestly answer the questions above? What are you most excited about and interested in?

⊚ ● EXPLORE FURTHER

(For more exploration, review the **bold-text** sentences in *IGIG* chapter 28, then answer the following questions.)

5. What have you been taught over the years about Heaven? How has your understanding of it changed over time?

6. Mark the following quoted passages in this chapter, and tell what they show us about what awaits us in eternity: Romans 8:18; 8:19; Luke 6:20–23; Revelation 22:3; Isaiah 25:7–8; Philippians 3:20–21; Proverbs 4:18; Hebrews 11:13–16; Daniel 7:18; 1 Corinthians 15:53; 1 Thessalonians 4:17.

7. In this chapter of *IGIG,* as you look over the bold-text statements, which one seems most important to you, and why?

●●● INVESTIGATE DEEPER

(For more intensive study, read *IGIG* chapter 28.)

8. Why is *beforelife* a better description of our existence in this world than *afterlife* is for our existence in Heaven?

9. What clearer and more realistic view of Heaven have you gained from reading this chapter?

10. Which stories or illustrations in *IGIG* chapter 28 did you find yourself most drawn to, and why?

11. Find the following passages in your Bible, and record the most important truths you see related to our future in eternity: Matthew 6:19–20; Luke 14:12–14; 2 Corinthians 4:17–18; 1 Thessalonians 4:14; 1 John 3:2; Revelation 21:1–3.

Hell: Eternal Sovereign Justice Exacted upon Evildoers
   (See also chapter 29 in *IGIG,* page 308.)

✦ FOCUS IN

When most people speak of the horrors of Hell, they talk as if it means the suffering of innocent people. That would indeed be terribly unjust—but nowhere does the Bible suggest the innocent will spend a single moment in Hell.

We rarely see *ourselves* as worthy of Hell. After all, we're not Hitler, Stalin, Pol Pot, Bundy, or Dahmer. Guilty people can always rationalize sin. Hell exists because sin has no excuse.

Hell isn't evil; it's a place where evil gets punished. Hell isn't pleasant, appealing, or encouraging. But Hell is morally good, because a good God must punish evil.

We cry out for true and lasting justice, then fault God for taking evil too seriously by administering eternal punishment. We can't have it both ways. Sin is evil. To fear and dread Hell is understandable, but to argue against Hell is to argue against justice.

✦ INTERACT

✤ In the Bible, Jesus spoke more about Hell than anyone else did.

Jesus referred to Hell as a real place and described it in graphic terms (see Matthew 10:28; 13:40–42; Mark 9:43–48). He spoke of a fire that burns but doesn't consume, an undying worm that eats away at the damned, and a lonely and foreboding darkness.

Christ says the unsaved "will be thrown outside, into the darkness, where there will be weeping and gnashing of teeth" (Matthew 8:12). Jesus taught that an unbridgeable chasm separates the wicked in Hell from the righteous in paradise. The wicked suffer terribly, remain conscious, retain their desires and memories, long for relief, cannot find comfort, cannot leave their torment, and have no hope (see Luke 16:19–31).

Our Savior could not have painted a bleaker picture of Hell....

Why do I believe in an eternal Hell? Because Jesus clearly and repeatedly affirmed its existence....

We cannot make Hell go away simply because the thought of it makes us uncomfortable. If I were as holy as God, if I knew a fraction of what he knows, I would realize Hell is just and right. We should weep over Hell, but not deny it. ✖

1. Does your understanding of Hell match what Jesus says about it? In what ways do you think your own perspective may need further development and deepening?

✖ The Bible teaches Hell is a place of eternal punishment, not annihilation....

One popular annihilationist position maintains that unbelievers cease to exist when they die....

Another view states that unbelievers are destroyed not at death, but sometime later....

People believe in annihilation because it doesn't seem nearly so bad as eternity in Hell....

Annihilation is an attractive teaching compared to the alternative—I would gladly embrace it, were it taught in Scripture. But though I've tried, I just can't find it there....

Although the doctrine of annihilation continues to gain ground among believers, Christians must realize that embracing this doctrine minimizes, or worse, eliminates altogether the horrors of Hell. This doctrine in its most popular form merely confirms what most unbelievers already think, that their lives will end at death, and therefore there's nothing to be concerned about. In contrast, the

Bible speaks of an eternal Hell as something that should motivate unbelievers to turn to God, and motivate believers to share the gospel with urgency....

If we are going to discard the doctrine of eternal punishment because it feels profoundly unpleasant to us, then it seems fair to ask what other biblical teachings we will also reject, because they too don't square with what we feel. And if we do this, are we not replacing the authority of Scripture with the authority of our feelings, or our limited understanding?

2. Why is there such appeal in the teaching that unbelievers experience annihilation after death, rather than Hell?

Doesn't our main objection to Hell center in the belief that we are far better than we really are? We may accept in theory that we're sinners; we may even be able to list some of our sins (though we can give quite good reasons for many of them). But we do not even begin to see the extent of our evil in the sight of an all-holy God.

If we regard Hell as a divine overreaction to sin, we deny that God has the moral right to inflict ongoing punishment on any humans he created to exist forever. By denying Hell, we deny the extent of God's holiness and the extent of our evil. We deny the extreme seriousness of sin. And, worst of all, we deny the extreme magnificence of God's grace in Christ's blood, shed for us on the cross. For if the evils he died for aren't big enough to warrant eternal punishment, then perhaps the grace he showed us on the cross isn't big enough to warrant eternal praise.

Suppose that

- God is far more holy than we realize.
- We are far more sinful than we realize.

If these premises are true—and Scripture demonstrates

they are—then why should it surprise us that God decisively and eternally punishes sin?

If we better understood both God's nature and our own, we would not feel shocked that some people go to Hell. (Where else could sinners go?) Rather, we would feel shocked—as perhaps the angels do—that any fallen human would be permitted into Heaven. Unholy as we are in ourselves, we are disqualified to claim that infinite holiness cannot demand everlasting punishment. ⚔

3. In your perspective and observation (of yourself and others), how true is it that our major objection to Hell centers in the belief that we're far better than we really are?

⚔ People commonly ask, "Why would God inflict infinite punishment for finite sins? Isn't that disproportionate punishment and therefore unjust?"

Scripture nowhere teaches infinite punishment; rather, it teaches punishment proportionate to the evil committed. The confusion comes in mistaking *eternal* for *infinite*. No one will bear in Hell an infinite number of offenses; they will bear only the sins they have committed (see Revelation 20:12–13).

The length of time spent committing a crime does not determine the length of the sentence for that crime. It may take five seconds to murder a child, but five seconds of punishment would hardly bring appropriate justice. Crimes committed against an infinitely holy God cannot be paid for in finite measures of time. ⚔

4. Do you believe Hell is an appropriate punishment for those who refuse to obey God? How does your answer reflect upon the character of God?

⊛ ● EXPLORE FURTHER

(For more exploration, review the **bold-text** sentences in *IGIG* chapter 29, and then respond to the following questions.)

5. What have you been taught about Hell? How has your understanding of it changed over the years?

6. Mark the following quoted passages in this chapter, and tell what they show us about Hell: Mark 8:36–37; Matthew 25:46; Revelation 14:11; 2 Thessalonians 1:9; Matthew 10:28.

7. In this chapter of *IGIG,* as you look over the bold-text statements, which one is most significant to you, and why?

⊛ ● ● INVESTIGATE DEEPER

(For more intensive study, read *IGIG* chapter 29.)

8. Because of what has happened on Earth, why does *justice* require the existence of Hell in eternity?

9. What clearer and more realistic view of Hell have you gained from reading this chapter?

10. Which stories or illustrations in *IGIG* chapter 29 did you find most compelling, and why?

11. Find the following passages in your Bible, and record the most important truths you find in them about Hell: Matthew 8:12; 10:28; 11:20–24; 13:40–42; 25:41; Mark

9:43–48; Luke 12:47–48; 16:19–31; 20:45–47; Romans 2:3–6; 2 Peter 2:4; Revelation 19:20; 20:10, 12–15; 21:8.

GOD'S ALLOWANCE AND RESTRAINT OF EVIL AND SUFFERING

(Links with section 8 in *If God Is Good,* pages 325–358.)

Why Doesn't God Do More to Restrain Evil and Suffering?
(See also chapter 30 in *IGIG,* page 327.)

❋ FOCUS IN

God may already be restraining 99.99 percent of evil and suffering. God may also be preventing 99.99 percent of disasters.

Why haven't tyrants, with access to powerful weapons, destroyed this planet? What has kept infectious diseases and natural disasters from killing 99 percent of the world's population rather than less than 1 percent? How much evil and suffering is too much? Could God reduce the amount without restricting meaningful human choice, or decreasing the urgency of the message that we need to turn to the Redeemer before we die?

Suppose we rated all pain on a scale of one to ten. God could reduce the worst suffering to level three, but then level three, now the worst, would seem unbearable. Any argument that judges God's goodness strictly by his elimination of pain will, in the end, not leave us satisfied if he permits any pain at all.

❋ INTERACT

❧ If God permitted people to follow their every evil inclination all the time, life on this planet would screech to a halt. ❧

1. How have you seen God's hand work to keep you from following your own evil inclinations?

✙ Isn't it likely that a kind and all-powerful God routinely prevents terrible tragedies in ways that we do not see and therefore do not credit as miracles?...

People who ask why God allowed their house to burn down likely never thanked God for not letting their house burn down the previous ten thousand days of their lives. Why does God get blame when it burns, but no credit when it doesn't? Many pastors and church members have experienced church splits, feeling the agony of betrayal and disillusionment. But where were the prayers of gratitude back when the church was unified? Our suffering seems extreme in the present only because God has graciously minimized many of our past sufferings. ✙

2. What prayers of gratitude do you think God wants to hear most from you today?

✙ Our birthright does not include pain-free living. Only those who understand that this world languishes under a curse will marvel at its beauties despite that curse. ✙

3. Describe what it means for you to see *both* the beauty and the curse in this world.

● ● EXPLORE FURTHER

(For more exploration, review the **bold-text** sentences in *IGIG* chapter 30, and then respond below.)

4. How much worse would you say this world could be than it actually is?

5. Glancing over *IGIG* chapter 30, look for the following quoted passages: 2 Timothy 4:8; Matthew 28:20; Hebrews 4:16. What encouragement do they offer us as we

await God's final resolution of the problem of evil and suffering?

6. In this chapter of *IGIG*, as you look over the bold-text statements, which one is most important to you right now, and why?

◉◉● INVESTIGATE DEEPER
(For more intensive study, read *IGIG* chapter 30.)

7. How would you summarize the best answer to the question in this chapter's title: why doesn't God do more to restrain evil and suffering?

8. Which stories or illustrations in *IGIG* chapter 30 did you find yourself most drawn to, and why?

9. Find the following passages in your Bible, and record the most important truths you find that relate to the question of why God doesn't do more to restrain evil and suffering: Daniel 10:12–13, 20; Romans 1:24–32; 1 Corinthians 10:13; 2 Thessalonians 2:7.

Why Does God Delay Justice?
(See also chapter 31 in *IGIG*, page 334.)

◉ FOCUS IN
God's is not a vending-machine justice in which a coin of righteousness immediately produces reward, or a coin of evil yields swift retribution. Packaged theologies seek to neatly account for everything, but as Job,

Psalms, and the prophets repeatedly demonstrate, that's not how life works.

Yet God doesn't delay justice as long as we often imagine. The wheels of justice may seem to turn slowly, but they turn surely. Some rewards of goodness and punishments of evil come in this life. And though ultimate rewards and punishments await the final judgment, considerable justice, both reward and retribution, gets dispensed immediately upon death, when God's children immediately experience the joy of his presence and the unrepentant suffer the first justice of Hell (see Luke 16:19–31). This means that the maximum duration of injustice experienced by any person cannot exceed his life span.

✹ INTERACT

✥ Since sin demands death (see Romans 3:23), if people are to live, justice must wait.

Throughout history God has delayed justice, both upon believers and unbelievers, to give them time to come to him, grow in Christlikeness, and trust him more deeply....

God's offer of grace requires that he postpone judgment against evil, to grant more time for people to respond to the gospel....

In a world with immediate justice, Christ could not have accomplished his redemptive work. He couldn't have gone to the cross, because God would have stopped or enacted the death sentence on every evil act leading up to it. Who would have remained to crucify him? A world with quick justice could never put to death a perfect being. ✥

1. What does God's choice to delay full and complete justice say about his character?

✥ We should wait patiently and live godly lives, knowing a relatively short time remains until God will make everything right.

Many passages promise reward in Heaven. During the delay between now and then, we store up rewards. Paul says, "Command them to do good, to be rich in good deeds, and to be generous and willing to share. In this way they will *lay up treasure for themselves* as a firm foundation for the coming age" (1 Timothy 6:18–19).

God promises his eventual intervention as a reward for his people's patience: "From of old no one has heard or perceived by the ear, no eye has seen a God besides you, who acts for those who wait for him" (Isaiah 64:4, ESV)....

Why does the call to patience about the Lord's coming justice immediately precede a warning not to sin? Because the same judgment that will bring us reward will also hold us accountable. Knowing that the Judge stands at the door should motivate us to repent now and live righteously until he comes through that door. ⚔

2. What actions and attitudes exemplify anticipation of Heaven and its rewards? Which do you need to incorporate into your life?

⊛● EXPLORE FURTHER

(For more exploration, review the **bold-text** sentences in *IGIG* chapter 31, and then respond to the following questions.)

3. Why is it sometimes so difficult for us to wait for God's justice to be fully accomplished?

4. In this chapter, find and mark the following quoted passages, and tell how they express both the certainty of God's justice as well as the tension we feel as we wait for it: Ecclesiastes 12:14; Acts 17:31; Jeremiah 12:1–2; Revelation 6:9–11; Luke 18:7–8; 2 Peter 3:9; 3:8; Lamentations 3:22–23; Mark 13:10; 2 Peter 3:11–12; Acts 3:21; Psalm

40:1–3; Lamentations 3:25; 1 Timothy 6:18–19; Isaiah
64:4; James 5:7–9; Galatians 6:9; 2 Corinthians 9:6;
Deuteronomy 32:35; 1 Peter 5:6; Galatians 4:4; Ephesians
1:10; John 5:28–29; Galatians 6:7.

5. Find also where Psalm 39:5 is quoted in this chapter. In
   these words of prayer from David, what is particularly
   important for us to remember?

6. In this chapter of *IGIG,* as you look over the bold-text
   statements, which one is most important to you, and why?

◦ ◦ ● INVESTIGATE DEEPER
(For more intensive study, read *IGIG* chapter 31.)

7. How would you summarize the best answer to the question in this chapter's title: why does God delay justice?

8. Which stories or illustrations in *IGIG* chapter 31 did you
   find most useful, and why?

9. Find the following passages in your Bible, and identify
   further perspectives on why God delays justice in this
   world: Luke 9:52–56; 16:19–31; Romans 2:5–6; 3:23;
   1 Corinthians 3:11–15; 2 Corinthians 4:17–18; 5:10;
   2 John 8.

Why Doesn't God Explain His Reasons?
(See also chapter 32 in *IGIG,* page 342.)

❋ FOCUS IN

Sometimes we make the foolish assumption that our heavenly Father has no right to insist that we trust him unless he makes his infinite wisdom completely understandable to us. This lays an impossible demand upon God, not because of his limitations, but because of ours. A physicist father bears no blame because he can't explain quantum mechanics to his three-year-old.

We lack God's omniscience, omnipotence, wisdom, holiness, justice, and goodness. If we insist we have the right, or even assume we have the capacity, to understand the hidden purposes of God, we forfeit the comfort and perspective we could have had in kneeling before his vastly superior wisdom.

He is infinite; we're finite. He's the Creator; we're the creatures. Shouldn't that say it all?

❋ INTERACT

✣ I hope you are finding help from reading *If God Is Good,* but I also hope it's clear that I'm not proposing shrink-wrapped answers. There are none....

What we call the problem of evil is often the problem of our finite and fallen understanding.

We assume God should answer our questions. But sometimes our questions can't be answered.

If the problem of evil were the only thing we didn't understand, our complaint might get sympathy. But we are veterans of not understanding, aren't we?...

Sometimes we couldn't understand the answer even if God explained it. Or God may have explained it in Scripture, but we fail to notice it or refuse to believe it.

Children don't understand why their parents won't let them stay up late, eat cookies in bed, or feed chocolate to the dog. They don't understand why we discipline them, make them clean their rooms, or take them to the dentist. One day, when they grow up, they'll understand.

And so will we. ❖

1. As you think about evil and suffering, what is one of the questions that "can't be answered," as Randy discusses above?

❖ The God of providence weaves millions of details into our lives and into all the lives around us. Maybe he doesn't have one big reason for bringing a certain person or success or failure or disease or accident into our lives; in fact, he may have hundreds of little reasons. In order to understand God's explanations, we would have to be God.

God has revealed just enough of himself to give us reasons for faith, but not enough to make faith unnecessary.

In Eden, God could have explained more to Adam and Eve. Certainly he could have enlightened Abraham more. But if God made himself so readily apparent in everyday life that we couldn't doubt him, it would change the nature of faith. We'd lack a vital element of character-building. God's daily intervention and appearance would overpower us. We would *have* to believe in him and thus faith would become impossible. ❖

2. In your own faith and character, where do you sense the most need to grow? How do you think any current hardships or suffering you're experiencing are contributing to that growth?

⊛● EXPLORE FURTHER

(For more exploration, review the **bold-text** sentences in *IGIG* chapter 32, and then answer the following questions.)

3. What are the mysteries that you would most like God to explain to you?

4. In this chapter, find and mark all the verses quoted from the book of Job. What's the important perspective they offer as to why God does what he does (especially in allowing evil and suffering)?

5. Also find where Isaiah 55:8–9 is quoted in this chapter. Why do we often find it hard to accept the truth that's taught in this passage?

6. In this chapter of *IGIG*, as you look over the bold-text statements, which one is most significant to you, and why?

◦ ◦ ● INVESTIGATE DEEPER
(For more intensive study, read *IGIG* chapter 32.)

7. How would you summarize the best answer to the question in this chapter's title: why doesn't God explain his reasons?

8. Why should we not be surprised by our inability to understand all of God's purposes in this world's evil and suffering?

9. Which stories or illustrations in *IGIG* chapter 32 did you find yourself most intrigued by, and why?

10. In what way does it honor God when we trust him, even when we don't understand what he's doing?

Understanding That God Is God and We Are Not
(See also chapter 33 in *IGIG,* page 352.)

✸ FOCUS IN

Of all there is to know in the entire universe, how much do you know? Let's say you're the smartest human being who's ever lived and that you know 1 percent (of course, nobody knows nearly that much). Is it possible that in the 99 percent you don't know, there exists or will exist enough goodness and happiness in the universe to outweigh all the evil and suffering?

Is it possible that in the 99 percent you don't know, a good God exists who has legitimate reasons for not making his purposes clearer and for not forcing people to recognize his existence? Is it possible that some rational explanation exists—if you were smart enough to understand it—for why this good God permits evil and suffering?

We reveal a staggering arrogance in assuming God *owes* us an explanation for anything.

✸ INTERACT

✖ What possible good can come from that deranged man murdering my uncle with a meat cleaver? Or the terrible accident that killed my nineteen-year-old friend Greg? Or my family members and friends who've wasted away from diseases?

I can't say that a commensurate good has yet come out of those situations. But I can say I have seen *some* good come through each of them, enough to give me faith that there may exist countless goods I cannot see....

Since we know that happens *sometimes,* couldn't it happen far more often than we realize?...

God calls upon us to trust him, that he will work all evil and suffering in our lives for good. We can learn to trust God in the worst of circumstances, even for what we cannot currently see—indeed, that is the very nature of biblical faith. ⚔

1. What are some recent examples in which you've seen something good result from suffering or acts of evil?

⚔ God is doing what it takes to create the greatest amount of ultimate good, even when, for now, that requires evil and suffering....

Shouldn't a good God do everything possible to ensure the greatest and most lasting good to those he loves? If he knows that a limited amount of evil, lasting a limited amount of time, can result in far more eternal good, then wouldn't he be morally justified in allowing it? Instead of condemning God for a plan that includes evil and suffering, shouldn't we commend him for it in light of the greater redemptive good it will forever accomplish? ⚔

2. Do you know of some people who would probably answer no to the questions above (maybe even yourself)? If so, what would be the reasoning behind that answer?

⚬ ● EXPLORE FURTHER

(For more exploration, review the **bold-text** sentences in *IGIG* chapter 33, and then respond to the questions below.)

3. In general, how well are you able to look beyond appearances to actual reality? How can we cultivate the ability to look not at what is seen but at what is unseen (2 Corinthians 4:18)?

4. Glance over *IGIG* chapter 33, looking for the following quoted passages: Numbers 23:19; Psalm 50:21; Romans 8:31, 39. How do they reinforce the truth that "God is God and we are not"?

5. What do you think are the most important functions that God should fill in a person's life?

6. In this chapter of *IGIG,* as you look over the bold-text statements, which one is most important for you right now, and why?

◉ ◉ ● INVESTIGATE DEEPER
(For more intensive study, read *IGIG* chapter 33.)

7. Why is it arrogant of us to assume that God owes us an explanation for anything?

8. What does it mean for us to "let God be God"?

9. Which stories or illustrations in *IGIG* chapter 33 did you find yourself most drawn to, and why?

10. Find these verses in your Bible and identify what they have to teach us about the meaning of *faith:* Hebrews 11:8, 13, 27, 32–39.

PART 4

Our Best Response

(Links with sections 9–11 and the conclusion in If God Is Good, *pages 359–494)*

Accepting God's Purposes

EVIL AND SUFFERING USED FOR GOD'S GLORY

(Links with section 9 in *If God Is Good,* pages 359–90.)

Pain and Suffering in God's World
(See also chapter 34 in *IGIG,* page 361.)

◈ FOCUS IN

Worse things can happen to us than dying young of a terrible disease. We could live in health and wealth, then die without Christ and go to Hell. To know Christ but fail to draw close to him is immeasurably worse than a disease that gets our attention and prompts us to look to him.

When Nanci and I passed through a particularly difficult period of our lives, we felt like we'd "done our time," as if we shouldn't have to face more difficulty for a while. But that's not how it works. As everyone living with ongoing disabilities, diseases, and heartaches knows, in this life God doesn't parcel out a certain amount of suffering so that once it runs out we'll face no more. But the promise remains: "Though he brings grief, he will show compassion, so great is his unfailing love" (Lamentations 3:32).

◈ INTERACT

❧ Suffering does not have a cumulative nature. The terrible suffering of six million people may seem six million times worse than the suffering of one. But no one, except God, can experience the suffering of six million people. All

of us remain limited to our own suffering. While our suffering may include an emotional burden for others who suffer,
it cannot grow larger than we are. The limits of our finite
beings dictate the limits of our suffering....

Consider that while our suffering can rise only to the
level we individually can suffer, Jesus suffered for all of
us. All the evils and suffering that we tell him he never
should have permitted, he willingly inflicted upon himself,
for us. �

1. How would you explain the differences between how *we*
   perceive and experience human suffering, and how God
   perceives and experiences it?

✖ I fell in love with astronomy years before I fell in love
with the Lord of the cosmos. Night after night I observed
the marvels of planets, stars, nebulae, and galaxies. As
every backyard astronomer knows, streetlights and bright
moonlight obscure the wonders of the night sky. In order to
see the full glory of the stars, I learned that you must stay
out for hours in the cold darkness. I did this night after
night because what I discovered was worth it.

As the Heavens declare God's glory in the absence
of other light, so God shows himself against the backdrop
of evil and suffering—if only we are willing to look...and
to discover that seeing him is worth even the cold
darkness. �

2. What are you currently learning most about God's glory?

⊛⊛ EXPLORE FURTHER

(For more exploration, review the **bold-text** sentences in *IGIG* chapter 34,
and then answer the following questions.)

3. What part does pain play in our suffering? Can there be suffering without pain? Why or why not?

4. In this chapter, mark the following quoted passages, and describe how they show that grief and weeping are common and healthy among God's people: 1 Thessalonians 4:13; Isaiah 53:3; Psalms 56:8; 119:28; Lamentations 3:32.

5. Find and mark where John 5:6 is quoted in this chapter. This verse includes a question Jesus asks; what is your own answer to that question, and why is that your answer?

6. In this chapter of *IGIG,* as you look over the bold-text statements, which one is most important to you, and why?

●●● INVESTIGATE DEEPER
(For more intensive study, read *IGIG* chapter 34.)

7. What is the best biblical explanation for why pain exists in our human experience?

8. Which stories or illustrations in *IGIG* chapter 34 did you find yourself most drawn to, and why?

9. Why is it important to understand that, as Randy says (on page 363), "suffering does not have a cumulative nature"?

Apparently Gratuitous Evil and Pointless Suffering
   (See also chapter 35 in *IGIG,* page 370.)

● **FOCUS IN**

Not *seeing* the point in extreme suffering doesn't prove there *is* no point. The very worst wrongs we know about can indeed seem utterly void of meaning and higher purpose. But at present, we seldom if ever can glimpse their full picture. After all, on that dark day when Jesus was tortured and killed, who among those that really knew him could see the tiniest thread of positive meaning in any of it? Yet that very crime brought more blessing and benefit for humanity, and more glory for God, than any other event in the universe's history.

Behind almost every expression of the problem of evil stands an assumption: we know what an omniscient, omnipotent, morally perfect being *should* do.

Since detailed past, present, and future knowledge is unavailable to us, we sometimes consider accidents random and pointless. We don't see that God has and will accomplish good purposes through them. Some good actions may result in great evils, while one tragic death may save the world from tyranny. Who but God is in a position to know such things?

● **INTERACT**

   ✣ God's goodness and sovereignty and his plan for the world...convince me that no evil is completely pointless. Yet...even if you believe in pointless evil and suffering, its existence does not in itself disprove an all-powerful and all-loving God....

   Some Christians believe God has specific purposes *for* suffering; others believe that he doesn't but still brings about certain good results *from* suffering. But if an all-knowing God determines in advance to bring about certain good results from suffering, doesn't that qualify as a purpose? And if God will not permit anything to happen that he can't use to glorify himself or bring ultimate good to his people, then even a terrible evil would not be gratuitous.

Evils such as rape and murder certainly *look* gratuitous. But are we qualified to say they really are? Didn't the violent, excruciating death of Jesus, when it happened, appear both gratuitous and pointless in the extreme? ✖

1. Do you agree or disagree with Randy's conviction "that no evil is completely pointless"?

✖ Only God is in the position to determine what is and isn't pointless.

Suffering may cause us to long for God to complete his redemptive plan. It may cause us to grieve for the human rebellion that caused suffering. If it does those things, it is not pointless....

As finite and fallen individuals, we lack the necessary qualifications to assess what God should and should not do. Not only do we know very little, even what we think we know is often distorted....

This we do know, according to God's Word: For the believer in Christ, this life's suffering, no matter how great, ends at death. Jesus paid a terrible price on the cross so that no person's suffering need continue beyond this life. ✖

2. Has your own experience of hardship and suffering caused you to long for the completion of God's redemptive plan, and to grieve for humanity's sin and rebellion that causes suffering? If so, in what ways?

◉ ◉ EXPLORE FURTHER

(For more exploration, review the **bold-text** sentences in *IGIG* chapter 35, and then respond to the following questions.)

3. What kinds of evil and suffering seem most pointless to you?

4. Find and mark where Romans 5:2–4 is quoted in this chapter. How does this passage indicate that our greatest satisfaction is commonly found in overcoming the most difficult challenges?

5. In this chapter of *IGIG,* as you look over the bold-text statements, which one is most significant for you right now, and why?

●●● INVESTIGATE DEEPER
(For more intensive study, read *IGIG* chapter 35.)
6. Why is there ultimately no such thing as "pointless" suffering?

7. Which stories or illustrations in *IGIG* chapter 35 did you find most compelling, and why?

How the Health and Wealth Gospel Perverts Our View of Evil and Suffering
(See also chapter 36 in *IGIG,* page 378.)

● FOCUS IN
This false worldview breeds superficiality, seriously misrepresents the gospel, and sets people up to believe when evil and suffering come to them that God has been untrue to his promises.

In some cases, pleasing God results in suffering.

Suffering shouldn't surprise us. God has promised it. One of the great tragedies about the health and wealth gospel is that it makes God seem like a liar. When people believe that God promises to keep them from suffering, God appears untrustworthy when suffering comes.

If you're a Christian, God will deliver you from *eternal* suffering. And even now he'll give you joyful foretastes of living in his presence. *That's* his promise.

⁂ INTERACT

✣ Prosperity theology has poisoned the church and undermined our ability to deal with evil and suffering.

Some churches today have no place for pain. Those who say God has healed them get the microphone, while those who continue to suffer are shamed into silence or ushered out the back door.

Paul had a much different viewpoint. "It has been granted to you on behalf of Christ not only to believe in him, but to suffer for his sake" (Philippians 1:29). "In the world you will have tribulation," Jesus pledged (John 16:33, ESV). We should count on these promises as surely as we count on John 3:16....

The health and wealth gospel's claims are so obviously opposed to countless biblical passages that it is difficult to imagine, apart from the deceptive powers of Satan, how so many Christians could actually believe them....

Christians should expect to suffer more, not less, since they suffer under the Fall *and* as followers of Christ.

If your goal is to avoid suffering in this life, then following Christ will not help you. Jesus himself said, "If the world hates you, keep in mind that it hated me first.... If they persecuted me, they will persecute you also" (John 15:18, 20). ✣

1. In what ways does prosperity theology poison the church and cripple Christians from effectively dealing with suffering?

✖ Medical and scientific advancements and spiritual claims of healing may convince us that suffering can and will be eliminated.

In an "it's all about me" world, we don't accept answers that entail our inconvenience, much less our suffering and death. We assume faith healing or medical breakthroughs can eliminate suffering and cure all diseases....

We do a disservice to ourselves and to others when we turn the avoidance of suffering and death into an idol.

Even if we don't end up dying from a particular disease or accident, all of us will die unless Christ comes within our lifetime. Have you noticed there are no 120-year-old faith healers? ✖

2. In your observation, how widespread is today's idolatry of health and long life?

✖ Prosperity theology encourages us to spend on ourselves the unprecedented wealth God has entrusted to us for relieving world suffering....

God has entrusted us with wealth that we may voluntarily distribute to those who need it most. Never have so many been in need. Never has God showered such abundance on Christians. When will we learn that God doesn't give us more to increase our standard of living, but to increase our standard of giving?

When we stand in his presence, Christ can show the scars on his hands and feet and say, "Here's what *I* did

about evil and suffering." What will we say when he asks,
"What did *you* do?" ⚔

3. How do you want to be able to answer the question in the
   paragraph above?

◉● EXPLORE FURTHER

(For more exploration, review the **bold-text** sentences in *IGIG* chapter 36,
and then respond below.)

4. What exposure have you had to the teachings of prosperity
   theology, and what has been your reaction?

5. Mark the following quoted passages in this chapter, and
   express how they contradict the health and wealth gospel
   (prosperity theology): Philippians 1:20–21, 29; John 15:18,
   20; 16:33; 2 Timothy 1:8; 3:12; Revelation 12:11; Matthew
   10:17–18, 21–22, 38; 1 Peter 4:12–13; Acts 14:22; Colossians 1:10–12; 1 Corinthians 15:31; Galatians 2:20.

6. Find and mark where Luke 7:4–5, 6–7, 9–10 and
   Matthew 8:2 are quoted in this chapter. These are instances
   when Jesus healed someone. Why do they not support the
   religious teaching that we can always demand and claim
   healing?

7. In this chapter of *IGIG*, as you look over the bold-text
   statements, which one has the most significance for your
   life, and why?

◉◉● INVESTIGATE DEEPER

(For more intensive study, read *IGIG* chapter 36.)

8. Why is it so important for us to resist attempts to solve the problem of evil by reinterpreting God and redefining the gospel?

9. Which stories or illustrations in *IGIG* chapter 36 stood out to you, and why?

10. What further perspective do the following passages provide on the teachings of the health and wealth gospel (prosperity theology): Deuteronomy 28:47–48; Job 1:18–22; Isaiah 11:6; 2 Corinthians 8:1–4, 13–14; 9:11; 12:7–10; Philippians 2:25–30; 1 Timothy 5:23; 2 Timothy 4:20; Revelation 22:3?

Why Does God Allow Suffering?

(Links with section 10 in *If God Is Good,* pages 391–446.)

How God Uses Suffering for His Glory
(See also chapter 37 in *IGIG,* page 392.)

◉ FOCUS IN

If you don't understand that the universe is about God and his glory—and that whatever exalts God's glory also works for your ultimate good—then you might consider God egotistical or cruel to test us for his sake. But the testing he does for *his* sake accrues to *our* eternal benefit.

God uses suffering to purge sin from our lives, strengthen our commitment to him, force us to depend on his grace, bind us together with other believers, produce discernment, foster sensitivity, discipline our minds, impart wisdom, stretch our hope, cause us to know Christ better, make us long for truth, lead us to repentance of sin, teach us to give thanks in times of sorrow, increase our faith, and strengthen our character.

God doesn't simply want us to *feel* good. He wants us to *be* good. And very often, the road to *being* good involves not *feeling* good.

⁕ INTERACT

⋈ Sometimes God intervenes by removing our suffering. Often he comforts us in our suffering. Sometimes he holds our hands as he brings us home to the perfect world he's made for us.

When someone survives an accident or gets a negative biopsy report, we sigh in relief and say, "God is good." We're right to give heartfelt thanks. But God remains just as good if the person dies or the biopsy report brings bad news. *God is good even when we can't see it.* ⋈

1. Why is it important (and right) to never doubt God's goodness? What difference should it make as we learn to do this?

⋈ We can give thanks in everything precisely because we have God's promise that in everything he works for our good.

If we have a big view of God, then we can see him at work all around us. We might thank any number of people for a particular thing; but ultimately we should thank our God of providence. ⋈

2. In your life, what gratitude toward God is overdue?

⁕⁕ EXPLORE FURTHER

(For more exploration, review the **bold-text** sentences in *IGIG* chapter 37, and then respond to the following questions.)

3. In this chapter, look for the following quoted passages: Isaiah 48:10; Revelation 3:19; John 9:3; Hebrews 5:8; Romans 8:29; 2 Corinthians 3:18; 1:8–9. What do they show us about how God uses suffering for his glory?

4. Also find and mark these quoted scriptures in this chapter, and explain how they show suffering to be part of our God-given destiny in this life: 1 Thessalonians 3:2–3; 1 Peter 4:19; 5:7.

5. Look for these quoted passages, showing us that suffering and evil cannot separate us from God's love: Romans 8:32; 8:38–39; Psalm 103:8, 13–14. What are the most significant truths you find in these scriptures?

6. In this chapter of *IGIG,* as you look over the bold-text statements, which one is most important to you, and why?

⬡ ⬤ ● INVESTIGATE DEEPER
(For more intensive study, read *IGIG* chapter 37.)

7. How does God use suffering for his glory? Explain it as fully as you can.

8. Which stories or illustrations in *IGIG* chapter 37 did you find most engaging, and why?

9. Find the following passages in your Bible, and tell how they indicate that God sometimes uses suffering to punish evil: 2 Kings 5:20–27; Psalm 32:3–4; Acts 5:1–11; 12:19–23; 1 Corinthians 11:27–32; Revelation 3:19.

How God Uses Suffering for Our Sanctification
(See also chapter 38 in *IGIG,* page 403.)

◉ FOCUS IN

People's suffering from natural disasters, diseases, wars, and accidents demonstrates sin's horrors. If life in a fallen world didn't sometimes show us such dreadful consequences of sin and its curse, we might look at sin and wonder, "What's the big deal?" Without a sense of the misery it produces, we'd have no motive to turn from it.

Sometimes we may resent God for imposing unwanted difficulties on us. If we see through the lens of eternity, however, that resentment changes to thanksgiving for making us better and ultimately happier people, even if it costs us temporary pain and extreme inconvenience.

The point is not the degree of evil intended against us, but our faithfulness in suffering. So regardless of why we suffer, God can use it to deepen our faith.

◉ INTERACT

✖ Armies and hospitals have chaplains, while political victory parties and Academy Award celebrations don't. Why not? Because hospitals and battlefields offer a clear view of death, while celebrations obscure it.

Death serves to draw our attention to what really matters—the state of our souls, and the God and people who will outlast this life. Death is a wake-up call, a reminder that our time here is fleeting and everyone's going to die. ✖

1. Is it morbid for a person to try to keep mortality in mind? Why or why not?

✥ We cannot understand evil and suffering without understanding creation, the Fall, and redemption....

Suffering exists because evil exists. God promised death would follow disobedience, and a world of death means a world of suffering.... To grasp redemption's meaning, we must see the devastation of the sin from which God redeems us.

Suffering, as sin's consequence, points us back to sin's ugliness. How horrible should we expect suffering to be? As horrible as sin. No less....

Suffering should prompt us to see our sin as a greater horror than the suffering sin causes.

While sin does not directly cause all our suffering, *if we were not sinners, our world would not know suffering.* Therefore, regardless of its reasons, both our suffering and that of others should always cause us to *hate sin.*

Though God tells us the wages of sin is death, he graciously delays sin's payday, giving us time to repent and turn to him for eternal life. But that very delay can allow us to live under the illusion that we are not such great sinners or that sin will go unpunished. The pornography addict will tell himself nothing is wrong until he ends up losing his job, his wife, and his children. He cannot gain freedom until he faces the horrific consequences of his sin. To hate suffering is easy; to hate sin is not. ✥

2. How does letting our suffering teach us to hate sin cause growth in our lives?

Satan wishes to destroy our faith through suffering; God desires to refine it....

Suffering brings us into deeper intimacy with God....

In the midst of our suffering..., God makes some of his most profound and precious self-revelations. Perhaps he does so because only then are we ready to hear them.

3. In what ways have you experienced greater intimacy with God through suffering?

● ● EXPLORE FURTHER

(For more exploration, review the **bold-text** sentences in *IGIG* chapter 38, and then answer the following questions.)

4. What does *sanctification* mean in the life of a Christian?

5. How does God use suffering for our sanctification?

6. In this chapter, look for the following quoted passages, then restate the evidence they offer that God uses suffering for our good: 1 Peter 4:13, 19; Job 19:26–27; Philippians 3:8; Matthew 28:20.

7. In this chapter of *IGIG,* as you look over the bold-text statements, which one is most thought-provoking, and why?

◉◉● INVESTIGATE DEEPER
(For more intensive study, read *IGIG* chapter 38.)

8. What's the best biblical answer to the question suggested by this chapter's title: how does God use suffering for our sanctification?

9. Which stories or illustrations in *IGIG* chapter 38 did you find yourself most drawn to, and why?

How God Uses Suffering to Build Our Character
   (See also chapter 39 in *IGIG,* page 413.)

◉ FOCUS IN
You may think, *I refuse to accept that suffering can prove worthwhile,* but your rejection of God's goodness will not make you better or happier; it will only bring resentment and greater pain. Accept health as God's blessing and its absence as God's severe mercy.

Suffering uncovers our trust in God-substitutes. God laments, "My people have committed two sins: They have forsaken me, the spring of living water, and have dug...broken cisterns that cannot hold water" (Jeremiah 2:13).

Let's be honest: virtually everyone who has suffered little in life is shallow, unmotivated, self-absorbed, and lacking in character. And yet we do everything we can to avoid challenges, both to our children and to ourselves. If we succeed in our avoidance, we'll develop in ourselves and our children the sort of character we least admire.

◉ INTERACT
   ✘ It seems counterintuitive to give thanks in suffering, but God commands it and countless people have benefited from it.

Getting in touch every day with God's grace, learning to thank him for the small things, serves us well when we lose big things. It deepens our reservoir and gives us eyes to see God's faithfulness and blessings at a time when we most need clear vision....

Expressing gratitude makes a grateful heart. Children who learn to say thanks become more thankful. Gratitude is a wonderful perspective-shaping habit.

Cultivating thankfulness today will allow us to cling to God's goodness and mercy in our darkest hours. Those hours lie ahead of us—but beyond them stretch unending millennia of inexpressible joy that we will appreciate more deeply because of these fleeting days of darkness. ✨

1. Why is it so important to cultivate thankfulness, and what are you doing to accomplish this?

✨ Suffering reminds us of our inability to control life....

We must relinquish our belief that we can prevent all bad things from happening. In a crisis we should lose our trust in the world and in ourselves, and cultivate our trust in God....

Diseases, accidents, and natural disasters remind us of our extreme vulnerability; life is out of our control....

We should repeatedly tell our Lord, "This house is yours. The money, this body, and these children belong to you. You own the title deed, you own the rights, you have the power of life and death."

It becomes much easier to trust God when we understand that what he takes away belonged to him in the first place. ✨

2. What has God done in your life to help you understand your inability to control it? What changes could you make in your lifestyle that would show your acknowledgment of his ownership of everything in your life? (See Randy Alcorn's books *Money, Possessions and Eternity* and *The Treasure Principle* for help in this regard.)

God uses disappointments and suffering to train us to share his holiness and righteousness.

Not all discipline is designed to correct sin. Its purpose may be to cultivate righteousness. An athlete doesn't train just to fix a problem; he trains *to improve his condition....*

Scripture promises, "God disciplines us *for our good.*" He doesn't miscalculate, doesn't make mistakes, and will never look back at what he brings and allows in our lives and say, "If I had it to do over again, I wouldn't do *that.*"

3. What training and discipline do you sense God is putting you through at this time?

EXPLORE FURTHER

(For more exploration, review the **bold-text** sentences in *IGIG* chapter 39, and then respond below.)

4. In this chapter, find and mark the following quoted passages, and tell what they teach us about the themes of gratitude and character building in the face of suffering: Psalm 105:1; 107:6, 8–9; 1 Thessalonians 5:18; 1 Peter 5:5; Philippians 3:10–11; Revelation 1:9; Job 23:10.

5. Look at these quoted scriptures in this chapter, and explain how they reinforce our need to learn the lessons that suffering

can teach us: 2 Corinthians 7:8–9; Luke 5:31; Jeremiah 2:13; Proverbs 18:10–11; 1 Timothy 4:16; James 1:2–4.

6. Find these quoted passages, which address our inability to own or control our lives: Psalm 24:1; Haggai 2:8; 1 Corinthians 6:19–20; 2 Corinthians 1:11. What important truths do we need to learn in this area, and why are they often hard for us to accept?

7. Look especially at Hebrews 12:7–11, which is quoted on page 422. Why are the truths and principles mentioned in this passage so important for us to understand in relation to our character development?

8. In this chapter of *IGIG,* as you look over the bold-text statements, which one is most significant for your life, and why?

⬡ ⬡ ● INVESTIGATE DEEPER
(For more intensive study, read *IGIG* chapter 39.)

9. Summarize what you believe is the biblical and best answer to this question: how does God use suffering to build our character?

10. Which stories or illustrations in *IGIG* chapter 39 did you find yourself most drawn to, and why?

11. In what aspects of your own character do you sense the most need for growth, and how do you think suffering might help to facilitate that growth?

Suffering Can Give Birth to Joy, Compassion, and Hope
(See also chapter 40 in *IGIG,* page 425.)

⊛ **FOCUS IN**

God permits rebellion while guaranteeing its failure. And what will rebellion buy in the meantime? A loss of joy—and for those who don't surrender to God, a *permanent* loss of joy in the world to come.

We harm no one through bitterness as much as we harm ourselves. Someone told me, "Bitterness is like drinking poison and waiting for the other person to die." In the face of evil and suffering, responding to God or others with bitterness, distrust, and accusations bears no good fruit. Responding in honest brokenness and turning to God in submission, faith, and trust yields untold riches of peace and comfort.

We're no substitute for God. But we do serve as his ambassadors. I heard Christian counselor David Powlison say that although God alone is the blazing sun, we can be three-watt night-lights. In darkness even a tiny light can bring hope.

⊛ **INTERACT**

✖ Scripture commands us to rejoice in suffering because of the perseverance it produces in us....

Adversity itself doesn't cause our joy. Rather, our joy comes in the expectation of adversity's by-product, the development of godly character. God doesn't ask us to cheer because we lose our job, or a loved one contracts cancer, or a child has an incurable birth defect. He tells us to rejoice because he will produce in us something money can't buy and ease will never produce—the precious quality of Christ-exalting perseverance.

Persevering is holding steady to a belief or course of action. It's steadfastness in completing a commitment....

God gives each of us a race to run. To finish well we must develop perseverance....

We rejoice in suffering in the same way that Olympic athletes rejoice in their workouts—not because we find them easy, but because we know they will one day produce great reward. �

1. How is God teaching you perseverance in the race he has given you to run?

✖ The comfort God gives us in our suffering prepares us to comfort others who suffer as we have.

One of God's purposes in our suffering is to prepare us to serve others, especially those who suffer as we have—for instance, from an addiction, miscarriage, abortion, infertility, divorce, or the loss of a spouse or child. Paul says, "The God of all comfort...comforts us in all our troubles, so that we can comfort those in any trouble with the comfort we ourselves have received from God" (2 Corinthians 1:3–4). The common ground of suffering breaks down barriers of wealth, education, vocation, and age. People in hospital waiting rooms often take an interest in one another's suffering and loved ones. They sail together on the same ship, riding the same rough waters. ✕

2. Who is "sailing on the same ship" with you, "riding the same rough waters"? Who can you give comfort to in their suffering, because you have experienced it as well?

⊛ ● EXPLORE FURTHER

(For more exploration, review the **bold-text** sentences in *IGIG* chapter 40, then answer the following questions.)

3. Glancing over *IGIG* chapter 40, look for the following quoted passages: Matthew 25:21; Romans 5:3; 8:24–25; John 8:31; 2 Timothy 4:7–8; 2 Corinthians 1:3–4; Galatians 6:2; Hebrews 2:18; 1 Corinthians 12:26; Psalm 30:5, 11–12. What specific benefits and blessings from suffering (and from perseverance in the face of suffering) do they point to?

4. In this chapter of *IGIG,* as you look over the bold-text statements, which one is most important to you, and why?

●●● INVESTIGATE DEEPER
(For more intensive study, read *IGIG* chapter 40.)

5. Summarize what you believe is the best answer to this question: how can suffering give birth to joy, compassion, and hope?

6. How would you explain the relationship between suffering, perseverance, and joy?

7. How does suffering increase our compassion?

8. How does suffering increase our hope?

9. Which stories or illustrations in *IGIG* chapter 40 did you find yourself most intrigued by, and why?

What We Can Do

How God Uses Our Suffering for the Good of Others
(See also chapter 41 in *IGIG,* page 436.)

❀ FOCUS IN

We want to serve from the power position. We'd rather be healthy, wealthy, and wise as we minister to the sick, poor, and ignorant. When those preaching God's Word have little personal familiarity with suffering, the credibility gap makes it difficult for them to speak into others' lives. But our suffering levels the playing field.

God uses the suffering we try to avoid to spread the gospel and build his kingdom. Jesus said, "I tell you the truth, unless a kernel of wheat falls to the ground and dies, it remains only a single seed. But if it dies, it produces many seeds" (John 12:24).

❀ INTERACT

✖ When I consider how both of my parents and my wife's parents deteriorated at the end of their lives, I might argue that it wasn't worth it. Although at times I saw a clear spiritual impact in each situation, still, it didn't seem like the upside outweighed the downside. But *seem* is the operative word. What *seems* and what *is* are often different.

Through our parents' weakness, my wife and I and other family members grew in character, compassion, and love. Suppose we could ask our parents now, in the presence of

Christ, "Were your suffering and your final years of indignity worth the character growth it brought about in you and your children and grandchildren and friends, and worth your and your family's spiritual impact on others, including caregivers?" I can picture them, in the universe next door, smiling and nodding emphatically.

1. In what difficult situations are you now most tempted to say, "It's not worth it"?

God called Christ to suffer for our atonement; he calls us to suffer for service and growth.

God doesn't call us to repeat Christ's atonement, but to accept it. He does call us, however, to deny ourselves, take up our cross daily, and follow him (see Luke 9:23). That involves saying no to present desires and plans in order to say yes to God and others....

We want deliverance from suffering. We don't want our loved ones to die. We don't want economic crises, job losses, car accidents, or cancer. Our prayers and often our expectations boil down to this: Jesus should make our lives go smoothly. That's what we want in a Messiah.

But it is not what *God* wants. Jesus is not our personal assistant charged with granting our wishes. While he sometimes does not give us what we want, he *always* gives us what we need.

Only when we regard suffering servanthood as our calling, as Jesus did, will we have the ability to face it as he did: "Consider him who endured such opposition from sinful men, so that you will not grow weary and lose heart" (Hebrews 12:3). "To this [suffering] you were called, because Christ suffered for you, leaving you an example, that you should follow in his steps" (1 Peter 2:21).

2. How exactly is "suffering servanthood" *your* calling? What is the specific suffering that you believe God wants you to endure, for his sake, as you follow in the steps of Jesus?

◈◉ EXPLORE FURTHER

(For more exploration, review the **bold-text** sentences in *IGIG* chapter 41, and then respond to the following questions.)

3. How has God used the suffering of other people to accomplish good things in your own life?

4. In this chapter, look for the following quoted passages: 1 Corinthians 9:22; Hebrews 11:35–38; 12:3; Philippians 1:12–14; John 12:24; Galatians 4:13; Luke 21:12–13; 1 Peter 2:21; Matthew 25:21. How do they address this topic of God using our suffering for the good of others?

5. In this chapter of *IGIG,* as you look over the bold-text statements, which one is most important to you, and why?

◈◉● INVESTIGATE DEEPER

(For more intensive study, read *IGIG* chapter 41.)

6. Summarize what you believe is the best answer to this question: how does God use our suffering for the good of others?

7. How can your experience of suffering make you a stronger witness for Jesus, and a more faithful and effective gospel messenger?

8. How can your experience of suffering cause you to be more faithful and effective in serving others?

9. Which stories or illustrations in *IGIG* chapter 41 did you find yourself most intrigued by, and why?

LIVING MEANINGFULLY IN SUFFERING

(Links with section 11 in *If God Is Good,* pages 447–85.)

Finding God in Suffering
(See also chapter 42 in *IGIG*, page 449.)

⊛ FOCUS IN

A woman self-consciously told one of our pastors that before going to sleep each night she reads her Bible, then hugs it as she falls asleep. "Is that weird?" she asked. While it may be unusual, it's not weird. This woman has known suffering, and as she clings to his promises, she clings to God. Any father would be moved to hear that his daughter falls asleep with his letter held close to her. Surely God treasures such an act of childlike love, for his Word represents his person.

The believers described in Faith's Hall of Fame (see Hebrews 11) all endured severe tests. None of them had an easy life. Yet they all clung to their belief in God's promises, trusting his goodness, and believing "that He is a rewarder of those who seek Him" (Hebrews 11:6, NASB).

⊛ INTERACT
✘ Clinging to Scripture sustains us through suffering....
Years ago I turned off talk radio when I drive, to listen to the Bible instead. Scripture on audio accompanies me as

I travel. I never regret investing my time this way—why listen to one more human voice when you can listen to God's? It prepares me to face whatever lies ahead. "Man does not live on bread alone but on every word that comes from the mouth of the LORD" (Deuteronomy 8:3). ✖

1. What new and better ways of "clinging to Scripture" would be helpful for you to try?

✖ Sadly, the doctrine of eternal reward is one of the most neglected teachings in the Western church today, partly explaining our failure to face suffering with greater perspective and to anticipate what awaits us in Heaven.

"Do you not know that in a race all the runners run, but only one gets the prize? Run in such a way as to get the prize" (1 Corinthians 9:24). Paul commands us to "endure hardship" and then gives the examples of soldiers, athletes, and farmers, each of whom has a goal in mind as he endures—victory, a crown, and a harvest (see 2 Timothy 2:3–7).

Jesus told suffering believers to "rejoice...and leap for joy, because great is your reward in heaven" (Luke 6:23). Greater suffering for Christ will bring us greater eternal rewards. ✖

2. How well do you understand the biblical doctrine of eternal rewards? How would you explain it in your own words, and what scriptures would you point to?

◦● EXPLORE FURTHER

(For more exploration, review the **bold-text** sentences in *IGIG* chapter 42, and then answer the following questions.)

3. In this chapter, look at the verses quoted from Psalms 13, 119, and 27 (on pages 449–51). How do they address this topic of our search for God in the face of suffering?

4. Look also at these quoted scriptures in this chapter: John 16:20–22; Romans 8:22; Isaiah 43:2; Psalm 16:8; Hebrews 13:5. What further evidence do they give of what God wants to do—and is doing—in our suffering?

5. Also find the following quoted scriptures in this chapter: Job 7:11, 16, 20; Psalm 22:1; Psalms 13; 73; Habakkuk 2:20; 3:16; Philippians 4:7; Habakkuk 3:19; Hebrews 11:25–26; 11:6; 2 Corinthians 4:16–18; Psalm 56:8. What additional perspective do they offer on this chapter's topic, and which of these passages have the most personal significance for you?

6. In this chapter of *IGIG,* as you look over the bold-text statements, which one is most thought-provoking, and why?

◦ ● ● **INVESTIGATE DEEPER**
(For more intensive study, read *IGIG* chapter 42.)

7. What can most help you focus on God when you're experiencing severe suffering?

8. Describe the comfort we find in God's promises, especially as we experience suffering.

9. What is the benefit that comes from looking forward to eternal rewards from God while experiencing suffering?

10. Which stories or illustrations in *IGIG* chapter 42 did you find yourself most drawn to, and why?

Finding Help in Dark Times
(See also chapter 43 in *IGIG,* page 459.)

⚜ FOCUS IN

Knowing that suffering will one day end gives us strength to endure this day.

Hope provides the light at the end of life's tunnel. It not only makes the tunnel endurable, it fills the heart with anticipation—a world alive, fresh, beautiful, without pain, suffering, or war. A world without disease, without accident, without tragedy. A world without dictators or madmen. A world ruled by the only One worthy of ruling (see Revelation 5:12).

Though we don't know exactly *when,* we do know for sure that either by our deaths or Christ's return, our suffering will end. From before the beginning, God drew the line in eternity's sand to say for his children, "*This much and no more,* then endless joy."

⚜ INTERACT

�֎ While I don't suffer chronic depression, I've had a few several month periods of depression that have awakened me to its reality and the hold it can have....

When I posted a blog about a time of depression I was experiencing, a few people expressed shock that someone who had written about subjects such as grace and Heaven could ever be depressed! I had to laugh, since far better people than I have experienced far worse depression, including Charles Spurgeon, Martin Luther, John Owen, and William Cowper, to name a few.

When I wrote about what I was learning from the depression, someone brought me a "prophetic word" that I was depressed because I wasn't trusting God. Ironically, I had come to trust God deeper in the midst of the depression than I had before it. God used that four-month period of depression to enrich my life. I hope I don't ever experience it again—but if I do, I pray he will enrich me through it again. ✘

1. What, if any, has been your own experience with depression, and what have you learned from it?

✘ Hurting Christians increasingly complain about the treatment they've received from church people. If you've had a bad experience, write out a list of what you wish church people had done for you and what you wish they hadn't done. Then use it as a guideline to reach out today and minister to others who need *your* wisdom and encouragement.

Don't grumble about others. Change yourself. Look closely inside the church and you'll find many believers way ahead of you in their care and compassion. Perhaps you haven't seen the church helping the suffering because you haven't stayed with the suffering enough to see what the church *is* doing. Many hurting people have told me amazing stories of faithful love shown by God's people in Christ's body. In hard times, Nanci and I have experienced the same. Imperfect as it is, we thank God for the church. ✘

2. How can you increase your connections with other people in your church, especially for the sake of encouraging them through their suffering?

✛ Even if God doesn't grant deliverance, we can pray persistently, with humble acceptance of God's will.

We should ask God to deliver us from Satan's attacks of unbelief and discouragement. We should learn to resist them, in the power of Christ (see James 4:7). Trusting God for the grace to endure adversity is as much an act of faith as trusting him for deliverance from it.

This does not mean God will always answer our prayers as we would like him to. Jesus pleaded three times for God to "Take this cup from me," yet God didn't. Three times Paul asked God to remove the thorn in his flesh, yet God didn't. Jesus and Paul both recognized God had higher purposes and willingly submitted to them. ✛

3. What do you see as the most important elements of our prayers during times of affliction?

✛ God's presence remains with his children whether we recognize it or not. In periods of darkness, God calls upon us to trust him until the light returns....

God sets a limit on evil and suffering in your life. In Job's life, Satan could do only so much for so long. God determined the limits. If you are God's child, then your suffering cannot outlast your lifetime. And since life continues after death, your suffering can last only the tiniest fraction of your true eternal lifetime. Rest in this knowledge. He offers you comfort before death and—one day—rescue *by* death or his return, whichever comes first. ✛

4. What is your attitude toward your own death? Do you have fear or anxiety about it? What do you expect it to be like?

We cannot have the right perspective in facing evil and suffering without a picture of the love-driven agony of Jesus on our behalf.

If the hands and feet of Jesus had not bled for me, I would not follow him. Since they did, by his grace I will follow him anywhere....

God's people have always put their own suffering in perspective by looking at Christ's.

5. What helps you to focus more clearly on the sufferings of Christ?

EXPLORE FURTHER

(For more exploration, review the **bold-text** sentences in *IGIG* chapter 43, and then answer the following questions.)

6. How do you see severe depression and suicidal thoughts as fitting into the problem of evil and suffering?

7. Mark the following quoted passages in this chapter: Romans 8:26; Psalm 34:18; Philippians 2:3–4; 2 Timothy 2:3; Job 8:21. How do these teachings relate to the right attitude and response for us to have toward depression and suicidal thoughts?

8. Find also the quoted words from Philippians 4:4–7 and Psalm 10:17 in this chapter. How can they help us be effectively prayerful in the face of suffering?

9. Also find these quoted passages: Psalm 30:5; Job 23:8–10; Daniel 3:16–18; Revelation 5:9–10; Hebrews 2:14–15. How do they help point those who suffer toward brighter days in the future?

10. In this chapter of *IGIG,* as you look over the bold-text statements, which one seems most important to you, and why?

⊛ ⊛ ● INVESTIGATE DEEPER
(For more intensive study, read *IGIG* chapter 43.)

11. If at some point in the future you experience severe depression or have suicidal thoughts, what are some of God's promises that will be helpful for you to remember?

12. In your own "dark times," what have you learned about God?

13. What is the right perspective for a Christian to have about depression?

14. What is the right perspective for a Christian to have about suicide and suicidal thoughts?

15. Why is prayer so important for lightening the load of suffering (our own or others')?

16. What does it really mean for us—experientially and practically—for God to "walk with us" in our pain? What does that look like? What difference does it make?

17. Which stories or illustrations in *IGIG* chapter 43 did you find most helpful, and why?

Finding Grace to Ease Others' Suffering and to Endure Our Own

(See also chapter 44 in *IGIG,* page 469.)

❊ FOCUS IN

To ignore someone's pain is to add to that pain. Instead of fearing we'll say the wrong thing, we should reach out to hurting people. Many times it's better just to put our arms around someone and cry with him or her; people almost always appreciate it when you acknowledge their loss. Yet so long as your heart is right, saying *something* is nearly always better than ignoring them.

"No test or temptation that comes your way is beyond the course of what others have had to face. All you need to remember is that God will never let you down; he'll never let you be pushed past your limit; he'll always be there to help you come through it" (1 Corinthians 10:13, MSG). This truth applies to every aspect of our lives, including the manner, timing, and duration of our dying.

❊ INTERACT

✖ There is a time for silence, to just sit and listen and weep with those who weep.

We often condemn Job's friends, but we should remember that they started well. When they saw his misery, they wept aloud. And then for seven days and nights they sat with him, in silence, wordlessly expressing their concern for him (see Job 2:11–13).

If we don't know what to say to a friend in crisis, remember that so long as Job's friends remained quiet, they helped him bear his grief. Later, when they began giving unsolicited advice and rebuke, Job not only had to deal with his suffering, but with his friends' smug responses, which *added* to his suffering.

When someone in pain expresses raw emotions, we shouldn't scold them. Friends let friends share honest feelings. When the premature and misguided correction of Job's friends hurt Job, they didn't have sense enough to say, "I'm sorry," and then shut up. They went right on hurting him. So Job said to them, "Miserable comforters are you all!" (16:2)....

Think of God's truths like tools. Don't use a hammer when you need a wrench. And don't use either when you need to give someone a hug, a blanket, or a meal—or just weep with them. ❖

1. What have you learned about the right ways to speak with someone who is in the midst of severe suffering or grief?

❖ Sufferers commonly ask, "Why me? Why not someone else? Why haven't my friends lost a child or their husband? Why can they walk and ride bikes while I'm in a wheelchair? Why have you treated me differently, God?"...

Comparison is poison. We shouldn't resent but rejoice for those who don't have our diseases or losses. We should thank God he knows exactly what suffering and death he's called each of us to endure. ❖

2. In your own experience, how have you seen that the kind of comparison Randy speaks of above can be poisonous?

◎● EXPLORE FURTHER

(For more exploration, review the **bold-text** sentences in *IGIG* chapter 44, and then answer the following questions.)

3. What do you think are the most important things we can do to help ease the suffering of others?

4. In this chapter, look for verses quoted from these passages: Psalm 88; Ephesians 4:32; Romans 12:15; Matthew 16:21–22; Ecclesiastes 4:9–10; 2 Corinthians 2:12–13; 7:5–6. What guidance and perspective do they offer regarding the right way to comfort others who are suffering?

5. Also look in this chapter for the following quoted passages: Job 40:8; Ephesians 4:27; John 21:18–19, 21–22; 1 Corinthians 10:13. What guidance and perspective do they offer to help us suffer well?

6. In this chapter of *IGIG,* as you look over the bold-text statements, which one has the most significance for your life, and why?

◎●● INVESTIGATE DEEPER

(For more intensive study, read *IGIG* chapter 44.)

7. From a biblical perspective, what do you believe are the

most practical and effective ways that we can help ease the suffering of others?

8. What do you believe are the most practical and effective ways that we can endure our own suffering?

9. How would you describe what it means to *suffer well*?

10. Which stories or illustrations in *IGIG* chapter 44 did you find most motivational, and why?

Discovering Death's Curse and Blessing
(See also chapter 45 in *IGIG,* page 479.)

◈ FOCUS IN
The last thing most people want to think about is the last thing they'll do: die.

Death is life's greatest certainty.

No exercise program, diet, or therapy prevents death. Corpses don't get cosmetic surgery. Even the young die from overdoses, accidents, and diseases. Famous athletes and Hollywood stars alike wind up in nursing homes. Suffering and old age are the great equalizers.

Two things stand between where we live now and that marvelous world where we'll live forever: death and resurrection. If we never died, we'd never be resurrected. We'd never enjoy a glorious eternity with Christ and our spiritual family.

So while death is an enemy and part of sin's curse, because of Christ's death and resurrection, it's the dark passage through which we enter the brilliance of never-ending life.

⊛ INTERACT

�֍ Death isn't the worst that can happen to us; for God's children, it leads to the best.

To die apart from Christ is terrible because it ends all opportunity and hope. To die loving Christ means spending eternity with God....

Dying is far better for the Christian than doing evil. It's much worse to deny Christ than to die. At death our sin will end and we'll be with Christ forever. Meanwhile, these words from a hymn make an excellent prayer: "O let me never, never outlive my love for Thee."...

Death is not a "natural" part of life as God intended it. It is the unnatural result of evil. And yet, God has removed the ultimate sting of death, which explains the appropriate sense of peace and triumph that accompanies grief at a Christian's memorial service. ✦

1. What has given you the most comfort during the loss of a loved one?

✦ We do a disservice to ourselves and to others when we turn death-avoidance into an idol....

Don't let discomfort or denial keep you from walking hand in hand with your family through the valley of death's shadow, where God can comfort and calm fears, where cups can overflow, and where you can celebrate and antici- pate God's eternal goodness and love.

Many people later regret not conversing directly and praying about death and Heaven during their loved ones' last days here. Don't be one of them. ✦

2. What does it mean to "walk hand in hand" with someone through the valley of death's shadow? What can we do to serve and comfort someone who is dying?

✣ My father showed more hostility to the gospel than anyone I've ever known. At age eighty-four, when he had a gun in hand, ready to take his life, God intervened. At last, in a hospital room before getting wheeled into surgery—suffering and desperate—he listened to the gospel I had tried to share with him over the years. I read to him from Romans 3, 6, and 10. God used his Word to break through to Dad's heart. Stunned but joyful, I heard my father repent, confess, pray, and entrust himself to Jesus as his Savior.

Four years later, Nanci and I, our high school daughters, Karina and Angela, and my brother, Lance, stood at Dad's bedside. We watched as his pulse monitor dropped from one hundred beats per minute, to ninety, then eighty, then steadily down to twenty, then went blank. My dad had departed the room, leaving his body behind.

Yet, because he had given his life to Jesus four years earlier—after God had used his suffering to bring him spiritual clarity—we said good-bye knowing we would see him again. That moment I'd dreaded for so many years— my father's death—brought me not only pain but an overshadowing peace and joy. ✣

3. In your own family or circle of friends, what non-Christians should you be regularly praying for, and seeking opportunities to share the gospel with?

⦿⦿ EXPLORE FURTHER

(For more exploration, review the **bold-text** sentences in *IGIG* chapter 45, and then respond to the questions below.)

4. How prepared are you for the day of your death?

5. In this chapter, look for the following quoted passages, and describe how they help us gain a healthy perspective

regarding death: Psalms 39:4–7; 90:10, 12; 2 Peter 3:13; Acts 8:2; 1 Thessalonians 4:13; Revelation 21:4; Ecclesiastes 7:2.

6. Randy says on page 482 that "for Christians, death is not a wall but a doorway." What does that mean?

7. What indications do you see in the world that a lot of people are not as aware as they should be of their mortality?

8. In this chapter of *IGIG,* as you look over the bold-text statements, which one has the most significance right now for your life, and why?

⦿ ⦿ ● INVESTIGATE DEEPER

(For more intensive study, read *IGIG* chapter 45.)

9. This chapter's title is "Discovering Death's Curse and Blessing." What exactly is that curse, and what is the blessing?

10. What are some ways we can prepare ourselves now for the moment of our death?

11. Which stories or illustrations in *IGIG* chapter 45 did you find yourself most drawn to, and why?

12. Find the following passages in your Bible, and list the biblical perspectives regarding death: Psalm 23; 1 Corinthians 15:19; Philippians 1:20–23; Revelation 21–22.

FINAL THOUGHTS ABOUT GOD, GOODNESS, EVIL, AND SUFFERING

(Links with the conclusion in *If God Is Good*, pages 486–94.)

⊛ FOCUS IN

In the end, Jesus Christ is the only satisfying answer to the problem of evil and suffering.

In fact, I'm convinced he's the *only* answer.

In this world of suffering and evil, I have a profound and abiding hope and faith for the future. Not because I follow a set of religious rules to make me better. But because for forty years I've known a real person, and because he willingly entered this world of evil and suffering and didn't spare himself, but took on the worst of it for my sake and yours, he has earned my trust even for what I can't understand. I and countless others have found him to be trustworthy.

He is "the Alpha and the Omega,…the Beginning and the End" (Revelation 22:13).

When it comes to goodness and evil, present suffering and eternal joy, the first Word, and the last, is Jesus.

⊛ INTERACT

✖ Telling yourself the truth about suffering can help you deal with it.

Suffering is limited. It could be far worse.

Suffering is temporary. It could last far longer.

Suffering, as we've seen, produces some desirable good. It can make us better people, and it can reveal God's character in ways that bring him glory and bring us good.

God can see all the ultimate results of suffering; we
can see only some. When we see more, in his presence, we
will forever praise him for it. He calls upon us to trust him
and begin that praise now. ⚔

1. What are the most important truths about suffering, evil,
   and God that you've learned in going through this study
   guide? Have you sensed any changes in your mind and
   heart, in your attitudes and actions?

● ● EXPLORE FURTHER

(For more exploration, review the **bold-text** sentences in *IGIG*'s conclusion, and then respond to the questions below.)

2. What continuing questions do you have about the problem of evil and suffering?

3. Glance over the text of *IGIG*'s conclusion, looking for the
   following quoted passages: Revelation 15:3–4; 16:5, 11;
   1 John 5:13; Romans 3:23; 6:23; John 19:30; Acts 4:12;
   John 14:6; Psalm 103:10, 12; 1 John 1:9; Romans 10:9;
   Ephesians 2:8–9; Malachi 3:16; Luke 12:3; Malachi 3:17–
   4:2; Revelation 21:4; 22:17; 22:13. What "wrap-up"
   thoughts and big-picture perspectives do they give us on
   addressing the problem of evil and suffering?

4. In *IGIG*'s conclusion, as you look over the bold-text statements, which one is most important for you to keep in
   mind, and why?

⊛ ⊛ ● INVESTIGATE DEEPER

(For more intensive study, read *IGIG*'s conclusion.)

5. What are some other factors nonbelievers should consider in evaluating whether there's a God, besides the problem of evil and suffering?

6. How will the future, as promised in God's Word, fully vindicate God in regard to the questions we have about evil and suffering?

7. Which stories or illustrations in *IGIG*'s conclusion do you hope to remember and possibly share, and why?

8. Find the following passages in your Bible, and record the most important truths you find in them—especially in the final "wrap-up" thoughts and big-picture perspectives they give us on addressing the problem of evil and suffering: Isaiah 59:2; Matthew 6:19–21; Mark 9:41; John 3:16; 20:31; Romans 4:12; 10:17; 11:20; 1 Corinthians 15:3–4, 54–57; 2 Corinthians 5:21; Galatians 2:20; Ephesians 6:16; Philippians 2:10–11; 1 Timothy 1:19; Titus 3:5; Hebrews 11:6; Revelation 20:12.

9. How do you think this study guide could help other Christians you know?

Group Leaders' Guide

You have a wonderful privilege and opportunity in leading a group through Randy Alcorn's *If God Is Good.* You'll be guiding men and women through a biblical exploration of an often troubling and bewildering topic—but one that brings invaluable comfort and peace when we truly understand it from a biblical perspective.

Here are some important points to keep in mind as you lead the group.

1. Remember that *the Holy Spirit and the Word of God are doing the teaching.* Do all you can to allow God's Spirit freedom to work through his Word in the hearts and minds of your group members. Don't burden yourself by thinking that *you* must be the instructor; free yourself by realizing that you're simply a facilitator of the group's discussion and mutual learning. You, and the others in the group, are an instrument for the Spirit to use to help everyone learn and grow.

2. *Keep praying.* Pray together before, during, and after each session. Pray regularly for the Spirit's enlightening help in everyone's hearts and minds. As topics of possible misunderstanding or controversy or disagreement are approached, pray that God's love and grace and truth will triumph. Pray that the group members will sense God's specific direction regarding the steps of obedience he wants each of you to take in response to your study and discussion together. Pray that you will be doers of the Word and not merely hearers (see James 1:22). Encourage prayer together as a group, while staying sensitive to the fact that some group

members might be uncomfortable with praying aloud. Promote an atmosphere where it's easy to grow in praying openly together.

3. Remember that the topics addressed by *IGIG* have often been confusing for Christians and non-Christians alike, leading to distorted thinking and many misunderstandings. Meanwhile, the personal pain often associated with our experience of evil and suffering can sometimes color our perspective and prevent us from seeing the bigger picture. We have much to learn and often much to unlearn in these areas. So be patient, allow the Holy Spirit to control the pace of learning, and proceed step by step, building steadily on the sure foundation of Christ and his Word.

4. If someone offers a perspective or opinion that isn't biblically accurate, here are some ideas to help you as a facilitator to steer the discussion in a positive direction:

(a) Deflect the topic to the group at large: "What do others of you think about that?" Those in the group who may be more mature spiritually should always feel the freedom to graciously and tactfully bring in helpful perspectives and biblical encouragement.

(b) Refer to Randy's perspective—not as a judge or umpire, but as a helpful viewpoint to consider. Most likely, any questionable perspective that someone mentions in your group will be something that's already addressed, directly or indirectly, in the pages of *IGIG,* usually with scriptural backing. Be familiar enough with *IGIG*'s content to be able to refer back to it when doing so will be particularly helpful and clarifying. Say something like, "That's something that Randy explores in *If God Is Good.* Let's hear his perspective on that, and interact with it..."

(c) Dialogue further with anyone who makes a questionable comment—not to "grill" him, but simply to explore together his perspective and see where it might lead. Ask clarifying questions to help the person sort out the logic and the implications of his or her viewpoint.

5. *Cultivate discussion.* Keep them talking, and get everyone involved. Do all you can to make sure each member in the group is comfortable with sharing thoughts and questions and feelings. Encourage and affirm everyone's contributions.

6. *Stay on track.* Watch out for tangents. Be ready to interject politely and refocus the discussion.

7. *Encourage application.* Encourage the group members to be aware of God's specific direction regarding the steps of obedience he wants each of you to take in response to your study and discussion together. Again, remember to be doers of the Word, and not merely hearers.

8. Be sensitive to your group's capacity and pace. Encourage further and deeper interaction with the *IGIG* content, while also recognizing the time limitations that will prevent some of the group members from doing this. Target your pace based on the approach you've chosen:

    * *Overview* (four weeks): The assumption here is that your group members probably will *not* dive into the actual text of *IGIG*, but will limit their focus to the quoted excerpts under the "Interact" headings. In this rapid four-week pace, the questions under the "Interact" headings will probably be all that you have time to discuss. But you can certainly encourage the group members to explore the other elements on their own, as they have time.

    ** *Exploratory* (eight weeks): The questions and instructions under the "Explore Further" headings are designed to help direct your group's attention to each chapter's content, especially the bold-text lead-ins as well as the numerous Scripture quotations. Make these the focal point of your discussion, after using the "Interact" questions to quickly get oriented toward each week's topic. The group members may not actually read all the text in each chapter, but encourage them to do so as they have time.

   ❋ ❋ ● *Intensive* (thirteen weeks): Help the group clearly understand that everyone is expected to read through all of the assigned text in *IGIG* each week. This will ensure your best discussion together.

Finally, since this study guide can be used in a variety of approaches and time frames, make sure everyone in the group clearly understands which parts of this guide they'll be doing week by week. Remember again the structure for each of the different approaches:

   ❋ *Overview* (four weeks): Each week you'll do one of the four main parts in this study guide.

      Week One—*Part 1:* The Burning Question
      Week Two—*Part 2:* Our Search for Solutions
      Week Three—*Part 3:* God at Work
      Week Four—*Part 4:* Our Best Response

   ❋ ❋ *Exploratory* (eight weeks): Each week you'll do half of each main part in this study guide:

      Week One—*1-A:* Something's Wrong
      Week Two—*1-B:* Tragic Choices
      Week Three—*2-A:* Alternative Answers
      Week Four—*2-B:* The Great Drama
      Week Five—*3-A:* Who's in Control?
      Week Six—*3-B:* Eternal Perspectives
      Week Seven—*4-A:* Accepting God's Purposes
      Week Eight—*4-B:* What We Can Do

   ❋ ❋ ● *Intensive* (thirteen weeks): Each week you'll do the study guide contents that correspond to each of the numbered sections in *IGIG:*

      Week One—Facing the Hurt and Confusion (corresponds to the introduction in *IGIG*)
      Week Two—*Section 1:* Understanding the Problem of Evil and Suffering

Week Three—*Section 2:* Understanding Evil: Its Origins, Nature, and Consequences

Week Four—*Section 3:* Problems for Non-Theists: Moral Standards, Goodness, and Extreme Evil

Week Five—*Section 4:* Proposed Solutions to the Problem of Evil and Suffering: Limiting God's Attributes

Week Six—*Section 5:* Evil and Suffering in the Great Drama of Christ's Redemptive Work

Week Seven—*Section 6:* Divine Sovereignty and Meaningful Human Choice: Accounting for Evil and Suffering

Week Eight—*Section 7:* The Two Eternal Solutions to the Problem of Evil: Heaven and Hell

Week Nine—*Section 8:* God's Allowance and Restraint of Evil and Suffering

Week Ten—*Section 9:* Evil and Suffering Used for God's Glory

Week Eleven—*Section 10:* Why Does God Allow Suffering?

Week Twelve—*Section 11:* Living Meaningfully in Suffering

Week Thirteen—Final Thoughts About God, Goodness, Evil, and Suffering (*IGIG* conclusion)

Printed in the United States
by Baker & Taylor Publisher Services